POSITIVE
PARENTING

Levi Coleman

POSITIVE PARENTING

HOW TO LOVE,
MOTIVATE, AND
DISCIPLINE YOUR
CHILD TO GROW
UP HAPPY AND
RESPONSIBLE

Don H. Highlander

WORD BOOKS
PUBLISHER
4800 WEST WACO DRIVE
WACO. TEXAS
76703

POSITIVE PARENTING

Library of Congress catalog card number: 79-63948
ISBN 0-8499-2887-7

Unless otherwise noted, all Scripture references
are paraphrased by the author from the standard
translations and the original Greek.

Quotation marked TLB is from *The Living Bible,
Paraphrased* (Wheaton: Tyndale House Publishers,
1971) and is used by permission.

Printed in the United States of America

With Gratitude

*All that we are and think and say comes from the enrich-*ments of our relationships with others, and from the positive ways they have touched our lives. Many have inspired and touched my life, and I thank all of you!

I'm grateful for all who have helped in bringing these ideas together. In particular, my appreciation to:

> *Emilie, my wife, for her love and partnership in life and parenting,*
> *Mary Elizabeth and Jennifer Emilie, my loving daughters,*
> *Don, Sr., and Genevieve, my positive and loving parents.*

It is to them that this book is dedicated.

And special thanks to Anne Christian, Joey Paul, and Floyd Thatcher, my editors, and to all of those at Word Books whose efforts helped bring this project to fruition.

—DON HIGHLANDER

Contents

Encouragement Is . . .

Painter Benjamin West's first venture into the arts could have ended in disaster. He was taking care of his younger sister Sally while his mother went shopping. Discovery of several bottles of ink inspired him to paint his sister's portrait.

Spilled ink and stray brush marks prevailed. Benjamin's intended work of art was a mess, and so was he. But when his mother returned, she looked past the ink blotches and stained furniture, picked up the piece of paper, and said, "Why, it's Sally!" She leaned over and kissed her young son.

Throughout his life, Benjamin West told of his special memory and turning point: "My mother's kiss made me a painter."

Simplistic? No, the essence of encouragement. Encouragement is:

—The feeling that comes when someone says, "I like the way you do that. Mind if I watch?"

—The confidence that I am loved for who I am and not just for what I can do,

—The knowledge that, no matter what happens, I'm accepted and needed as an indispensable part of my family,

—The assurance from someone I love that it's all right if I make a mistake because that's the way I learn,

—The conviction that I as a person am more important than the problems I get involved in,

—The acceptance of an honest appraisal that leaves me challenged to grow rather than condemned to fail.

Children look to parents for love, acceptance, warmth, and understanding. Those who have ever felt left out, misunderstood, or unaccepted know the need for encouragement. Encouragement cultivates enriching values and goals in life. It builds healthy self-esteem, self-confidence, and good behavior. Discouragement, on the other hand, breeds disappointment, dissatisfaction, dejection, and frustration. A leading child psychiatrist, Rudolf Dreikurs, insists that "a misbehaving child is a discouraged child."[1] He strongly asserts that encouragement is more important than any other aspect of child-rearing.

When we look to the Bible for help in rearing children who are spiritually alive, intellectually alert, and emotionally secure, we find that it instructs:

> Fathers, don't push your children to anger or resentment through unreasonable blame or commands, but raise them in the teaching and discipline, *encouragement,* and correction of the Lord (Eph. 6:4).

> Fathers, don't irritate, scold, or overcorrect your children to angry feelings, lest they become *discouraged* and quit trying. . . . it will break their spirits and they will feel harassed, inferior, and frustrated (Col. 3:21).

The biblical model of an effective Christian parent is an encouraging parent.

But being an encouraging parent is not always easy. No one has all the answers to the many questions about rearing children; we have all felt the pain of failure in attempts to be "the perfect parent." One reason for this is that children come during the busiest time of our lives. We're still discovering our own identities, making the right friends, working long hours, looking for the right place to live, finding the right things to enjoy. We're still feeling the need to grow and to enjoy being persons, adults, and marriage partners. Unless we make an effort, our children simply become additional baggage carried along the way.

We don't want that. We want to be *responsible parents* because we want to be responsible people, and because responsible parenting produces responsible children. We want to become sources of enrichment, encouraging our children by helping them become the persons God desires them to be.

Becoming such encouraging and responsible parents calls for the commitment and will power to turn impulsive reactions into constructive actions. It means making the choice for personal growth in the midst of struggle and adversity. It means searching for resources within ourselves and our environment, while we depend on God's strength, to help us reach our goal, and it also means learning how to apply biblical principles for living to the exacting responsibility of bringing up children "in the ways they should go" (Prov. 22:6).

It is my hope that this book will be of help in this process. The purpose of this study is to teach some of the skills which can help us all achieve these objectives:

1. To increase in understanding of ourselves, our families, and our children,
2. To learn how to build self-esteem through the use of encouragement,
3. To improve the marital and family communication process,
4. To learn how to discipline with love and authority,
5. To become growing, encouraging, sensitive, responsible parents who know how to encourage a child toward full emotional and spiritual maturity.

One day our children will look back and reflect and pass judgment on the way they were reared. What memories will they recall? Perhaps . . .

"Dad said I'd never make it, but I showed him."

"Mother told me I was no good, and she was right."
"There must be something wrong with me, because my
parents never trusted me."

Or . . .

"One thing I always knew was that my parents loved me
and believed in me, no matter what."
"My mother and father seemed to know when I needed
acceptance instead of condemnation. They were always
an encouragement to me."

We as persons are continually in the process of growing, changing, and assuming responsibilities. Learning to become *encouraging parents* is an important part of our growth process. And in that process we'll become *encouraged* and *responsible* parents as well.

1 | *Growing A Family*

**ESTABLISHING
GOALS FOR
MEANINGFUL
RELATIONSHIPS**

A successful business executive and his wife came to me for counseling, seeking to work through some of their family problems. During the course of our conversation, the man made reference to the thousands of dollars his company spent yearly for corporate growth research. Much evaluation, planning, developing of new markets, goal setting, and training occurs before expansion is implemented in most companies. Relating to that fact, I asked the husband what goals he had for his personal life and family. He stared at me with astonishment, then finally replied, "You know, Don, in twelve years of management I've never once given thought to working on goals for my personal and family growth."

Business has long recognized that making evaluations and setting goals is necessary for growth. The same is true for families. Few couples *plan* to have a mediocre marriage and family life. But many drift into it because they *don't* plan! The purpose of this chapter is to examine some of the purposes and possibilities of families, and to help us evaluate ourselves and set realistic objectives for personal and family growth.

WHAT IS A FAMILY FOR?

Families are the home base for developing healthy personalities and healthy relationships. In their book, *How to Handle Pressure,* Clyde and Ruth Narramore pointedly express the impact of family relationships upon personality development:

> There's nothing in this world that has as much influence on people as other people. People bring each other joy as well as heartache. They help, and they hinder. They have the capacity to encourage, or discourage; they can build, or they can destroy. . . .
>
> The closest unit in human experience is the family. It stands to reason, then, that family members influence one another in countless ways. Your habits, your thinking, your health, and most of all, your emotions are all affected by the relationships you share with the rest of your family.[1]

In order to grow, a family needs to operate and share together with a minimum of conflict. Mutual respect, fun activities, a sense of belonging, love, open communication—the basic ingredients for building positive relationships—are essential to the growth process. Each person needs the freedom to grow as an individual while learning to cooperate for everyone's best interest. Each member needs to feel accepted and worthwhile.

As children grow older, outside influences overwhelm them with pressures. Peer groups, school, and jobs make demands on them. Parents are also under pressure from the outside. The family needs to be a resource for processing life's complexities. But too often the family itself is a source of irritation and discouragement!

TWO BECOME ONE

A minister once instructed a couple that they needed to grow together and "become one" with each other. The wife replied, "Yes, pastor, but which one?"

When two people marry, each brings to the marriage his or her own basic objectives, family values, and ideas about child-rearing (probably based on the way each was reared). For this reason, it's often difficult for them to agree on specific methods and actions, to work in "oneness."

Children further complicate the situation. Each child strives to find his place of acceptance within the family. He uses a variety of efforts to meet his needs and reach his personal goals. He can creatively outwit his parents at times and keep them confused and bewildered. He often challenges their control over him and seeks to get others to serve him.

To preserve unity and order in the family system, parents must learn to communicate between themselves as to how they want to "grow" their family. Setting goals, following a plan, and learning to relate to each other and to children at each stage of development greatly reduces the amount of frustration in daily living. And goals weld families together. A home in which family members are working together toward common objectives is the kind of home which provides children with the warmth, acceptance, love, sense of togetherness, values, and models they need for living successfully and relating to others.

TAKING STOCK

The exercises at the end of this chapter are intended to guide the process of evaluation and goal-setting, and to provide a forum for communication between parents about personal goals and objectives. Each exercise is intended to be completed separately and then shared (single parents may want to discuss the exercises with a friend or with their older children). Parents may want to repeat the exercises at the conclusion of this study, to measure their personal and family growth:*

A FINAL NOTE

Family growth is a process. Growth takes time and involves constant change. Goals and objectives will not remain the same over a period of time, and not all personal and family goals will be achieved. The important thing is to keep reading, learning, experiencing, evaluating, and setting new realistic goals around which everyone in the family can draw together.

---

*Those willing to participate in a research study please send copies of your responses to Family Life Research, PO Box 422, Pine Lake, Georgia 30072.

FAMILY INVENTORY

Exercise #1: What are the greatest problems involving rearing children that you face in your family? At this point make a personal list of problems or difficulties you face as a parent. Then choose the three most important of these problems and list them according to priority. Share your list with your partner and compare with his or her list.

We feel most concerned about:

1.   1.

2.   2.

3.   3.

Exercise #2: What kind of a parent do you want to become? Talk together and state three specific goals each of you has for yourself. How can you begin to change?

Our personal parenting goals are:

1.   1.

2.   2.

3.   3.

Exercise #3: Now attempt to determine three family goals that the two of you share.

Our specific combined family goals are:

1.

2.

3.

2 | *Now That I'm a Parent, Who Am I?*

UNDERSTANDING
OURSELVES
AS PEOPLE AND
AS PARENTS

How do we become the kind of responsible, encouraging parents we want to be? The starting place is attempting to better understand ourselves as individuals and our role as parents. When we understand ourselves, we can begin to understand our children. After all, they are inheritors of our physical characteristics, attitudes, emotions, and values.

MADE IN GOD'S IMAGE

The foundation for understanding ourselves is understanding that mankind is made in the image of God. This is stressed four times in the first chapter of Genesis—we are made in God's likeness. What does this mean? We're not divine, all-powerful, all-knowing, or sinless like God is. But we're like God in other important ways:

God communicates . . . . we communicate
God chooses . . . . we choose
God thinks. . . . . we think
God is creative . . . . we can be creative
God loves . . . . we are able to love
God is a Person . . . . . . and we are persons

Furthermore, the Bible teaches that each person is very important to God. Because we are persons created in God's image, we possess great worth. Each of us is unique in all his creation; regardless of social status, race, intelligence, achievement, virtue, failure, success, or any other quality, we are each personally important to God.

Because of God's design, image, or pattern within us, we all have built-in needs and ambitions to be creative, communicative, loving, and just. We need freedom to make choices, assume responsibility, solve problems, and experience meaning in life. We all have physical drives—for food, sex, and self-preservation—but we are so designed that when we ignore spiritual values, when self-interest preoccupies our choices, we soon become restless and empty, driven to frustration and despair. Our needs and potentials as humans can never be fully realized unless we are rightly related to God, to ourselves, and to others.

PARENTS ARE "BECOMERS"

God has designed within us both the need and the potential for *becoming* all we were meant to be—totally fulfilled people. Recognizing that we are "people in process" can increase our understanding of ourselves, as well as of our children.

The question here is not what we intend for ourselves, but what God intends for us to become, in dependence upon him. C. S. Lewis, in *Mere Christianity,* paraphrases a parable told by George MacDonald:

Imagine yourself as a living house. God comes in to rebuild

that house. At first, perhaps, you can understand what He is doing. He is getting the drains right and stopping the leaks in the roof and so on. You knew that those jobs needed doing and so you are not surprised. But presently He starts knocking the house about in a way that hurts abominably and does not *seem* to make sense. What on earth is He up to? The explanation is that He is building quite a different house from the one you thought of—throwing out a new wing here, putting on an extra floor there, running up towers, making courtyards. You thought you were going to be made into a decent little cottage, but *He is building* a palace. He intends to come and live in it Himself.[1]

Transforming a cottage into a palace costs. But the initial price has already been paid by God, through Jesus Christ, and the process of rebuilding is underway in every committed Christian. We can be "confident of this very thing, that he who began a good work in you will carry it on to completion. . . ." (Phil. 1:6).

Commitment to God through Jesus Christ shapes our response to God's provision for growth experiences. Growth and change are not options for us. God wants us to be whole, fulfilled, growing. He has given his Holy Spirit to live within the human personality in order to bring about supernatural growth and change when the physical nature militates against the goal of spiritual, emotional, and psychological maturity. The changes he makes are changes within us—new values, ideas, beliefs, capacities, and purpose. We are always in the process of becoming new people *in him*.

NOBODY'S PERFECT

Realizing that we are created in the likeness of God with the potential to become all that he has planned is vital to our self-understanding. But being "becomers" means that we have not yet arrived. An important part of understanding ourselves is getting rid of the preconceived belief that we must be perfect parents if our children are to be healthy and happy. The perfect parent just doesn't exist. Being "be-comers" means learning to reduce the frequency and seriousness of our parenting failures, not ceasing to make mistakes altogether.

When we look at parenting this way, we can accept our failures as learning experiences. Understanding our failures and taking positive action to correct them will help us grow spiritually and personally. When our children see us dealing responsibly with our own undesirable attitudes and actions, they will be likewise encouraged to deal with their failures positively. Failing to admit and accept our negative be-havior, especially for the sake of preserving a "perfect parent" facade, only increases the potential for parent-child conflict.

Part of learning to accept our shortcomings as people and as parents is learning to deal constructively with guilt feelings. Guilt will not produce growth, and it can be used as an excuse to avoid change. As Christians, we believe that God knows we are not perfect, and that he forgives us our imperfections. Guilt can be a form of pride in refusing to accept that forgiveness. Guilt feelings, because they refuse to trust God for the present, work against our goals of growth as parents and as persons.

MEMORIES ARE RESOURCES FOR SELF-UNDERSTANDING

An important part of understanding ourselves as people and as parents is recognizing that past experiences have a bearing on our present attitudes and behavior. All that we have perceived and experienced since birth has been "re-corded" in our conscious and unconscious memories. These memories are important keys to the present. Accepting our feelings about our pasts, especially about our parents and families, can help us understand why we react in family situations as we do.

Childhood was our introduction to life. From our initial relationships we developed our early identities. We imitated those who were close and significant to us. We learned to react to the way others saw us, treated us, and responded to us. Many of our present ideas about ourselves, the world around us, love, money, sex, family, work, and leisure were derived from our early childhood experiences. These ideas may have been reinforced or modified later in life, but they remain basic to our self-perceptions.

We bring into our present family situations these preconceived ideas from our own childhoods; we tend to model our parenting styles after those we observed in early life. Present relationships are affected by our tendency to fall into old patterns stored in our memory banks.

Often we are amazed by our actions and attitudes, which seem at the same time so foreign and yet so much a part of us. When our behavior is desirable, we marvel at how well we're handling things. When we act or react in ways we dislike, we feel defeated and guilty. The situation becomes more complex and confusing when our spouses come from different backgrounds and find themselves parenting in ways frighteningly different from what they expected of themselves or of us. Parents and children both can be caught in a crossfire of confusion and frustration.

This is not to say that we are helpless victims of our memories—or "recorded scripts," as some refer to them. We are free to learn how to respond and choose between the conflicting options within us, once we have recognized the sources of our behavior. Some of the techniques suggested in subsequent chapters can help us in this process of becoming the kind of parents we want to be.

A PERFECT MODEL

As we have discussed, God has made us in his image, and desires us to be "becomers." He does not expect perfection from us, nor does he leave us at the mercy of our past memories. He gives us an example to follow, a perfect model to demonstrate encouraging, loving parenthood. Paul, in writing to the Ephesians, suggested that they

should "become imitators of God, as well-loved children of
the Father" (5:1). One paraphrase states, "Follow God's
example in everything you do just as a much loved child
imitates his father" (Eph. 5:1, TLB).

Some people who have bad "parent scripts" have trouble
with this concept. It has been said that Martin Luther's
father was so stern with him that for the rest of his life
Luther found it difficult to pray, "Our Father." In his mind
the word *father* stood for nothing but severity.

So if God is to be perceived as the model for the Christian
parent, we must correct any misconceptions about him we
have picked up from our past experiences. And if we are
created in the image of God, we can know more about
ourselves as we know more about God.

God is above all our loving Father. Love distinguishes the
Christian God from all others. Fatherhood suggests loving
provision, kindness, protection, unlimited mercy, warmth
and affection, correction, and loving restriction. Fatherhood also indicates "ownership" or "belonging to." God
adopts us as his very own when, through Christ, we become
part of his spiritual family. We are related to him through
our personal faith in his Son. Acknowledging the God of
the Bible as Father gives us a basis for self-respect. We are
worth a lot to him.

God is an encouraging Father. He does not deal with us
solely on the basis of our actions, but also on the basis of
our needs. When we are in trouble, he sees past the
immediate situation to understand the reasons for our
distress. And in Christ he meets us with grace, love,
acceptance, and correction—all in a manner that encourages right attitudes and actions. God is both supportive and
consistent. Out of a loving and just nature, he has established controls that provide the right balance between
freedom and restraint. God is accessible, approachable, and
reachable. He responds to our need for love and guidance
and is both firm and kind in the way that he communicates
with us.

When we begin to understand how God deals with us in
tender, loving encouragement, we understand our value to

him. And we see the *model* of the kind of relationship we are to have with our children.

PARENTING STYLES

As we continue to try to understand ourselves as parents and to find constructive ways to relate more meaningfully to our children, we must honestly evaluate the way we conduct ourselves as parents—our parenting style. We need to get a picture of what kind of parents we are now if we want to progress toward becoming the kind of parents we want to be. As we begin to understand our tendencies as parents, we can learn more appropriate skills for being effective, encouraging parents.

It has been reported that 95 percent of family-life research has been based on what makes families sick, rather than on what makes them well. The emphasis of this book is on the latter—what makes families healthy. Yet we want to take a brief, clear look at four unhealthy parenting styles before examining in depth the fifth, healthy style—the style that is the subject of the rest of the book.

As we look at the four negative parenting styles presented here, it is important to reflect seriously on parenting roles and to identify beliefs and behavior honestly. Here are some questions to ask: "What do I do that is similar to how my parents dealt with conflict and discipline? What makes me different from them? What habits or traits are characteristic of the image my child has of me?" It is possible that one parent may use more than one style, although most find themselves falling in one category more than the others.

Negative Parenting Style #1: The Critical Parent.

Nine-year-old Johnny was almost finished with his school project paper. Dad asked to look at it. Johnny was reluctant to hand over the paper, but Dad insisted.

"Just as I expected," he said. "Won't you ever learn to be neat? If I were your teacher, I'd make you do it over. You're the sloppiest kid I've ever seen. Look at the misspelled words. Just stop where you are and start all over."

Sherry gets it when she goes shopping with her mother.
"Oh no, dear. That looks horrible. No, not that color.
When will I ever teach you good taste?"

The critical parenting style is based on the attitude that
the parent is always right and the child is always wrong.
Critical parents blame in order to avoid changing their own
behavior; they use ridicule, sarcasm, or harsh words to
express their frustrations. The focus is always on their
children's shortcomings rather than on their assets. All this
criticism, nagging, name-calling, or ridicule would be devas-
tating to anyone, but it is particularly disastrous to children,
who are in the process of developing a sense of self-worth.

Criticism can take the form of guilt-producing moralistic
preaching: parents, operating under the delusion that guilt
will motivate children to change, try to make them feel bad
about their behavior, feelings, or ideas. Critical parents
have a vocabulary that is limited to nonaffirming words like
*should, shouldn't, must, must not, always, never, can't,
ought,* and *ought not.* They rationalize, moralize, lecture,
argue, and judge, usually in a punitive tone of voice. The
atmosphere in the home is often charged with distrust and
disrespect.

Negative Parenting Style #2: The Permissive Parent.

Permissive parents go to the opposite extreme. They want
to be "good parents," either doing everything for their
children or allowing them to do anything they want. Little is
expected of the children, and they are seldom corrected.
The parents may take great pleasure in giving their children
all the things they wanted when they were small and did not
get.

"Smothering a child with love" and serving his or her
every whim may come from the parents' inability to
confront behavioral issues squarely. Or the parents may be
overly concerned with making the children feel happy.
Whatever the cause, the result is the same: children who
grow up selfish and unhappy, without self-discipline or self-
respect.

Negative Parenting Style #3: The Controlling Parent.

Controlling, over-caring parents try desperately to be

perfect parents. Such parents make sure their children get up on time, dress properly, be on time everywhere, be involved in all activities. The child doesn't have to assume responsibility for anything; the parent takes on all responsibility:

"Don't be late."
"Clean your shoes."
"Put your coat in the closet."
"Hang up your clothes."
"Don't forget your books."
"Go to bed."

Every move is supervised by the parents, who feel compelled to be competent. Unlike critical parents, controlling parents tell the children precisely what to do and how to do it before they have the opportunity to do it wrong.

The controlling parenting style produces emotional fatigue in the parents and irresponsibility in the children. Children who have controlling parents grow up unprepared for reality living and face disillusionment. They have no chance to develop self-confidence.

Negative Parenting Style #4: The Commanding Parent.

Commanding parents may be harsh or loving, excitable or calm, loud or quiet. But their goal is always the same—keeping everyone and everything under their command.

Like critical parents and controlling parents, commanding parents are perfectionists. They maintain a "shape up or ship out" attitude. Threats, orders, commands, demands—all insist that parents are superior and children are mere subordinates. Children "submit" under the pressure of feeling inferior or worthless rather than out of respect and responsibility.

Parents who fit this style tend to be *authoritarian,* but not necessarily *authoritative.* Parents who speak with authority earn respect and cooperation by example. Authoritarian parents, on the other hand, expect children to submit to an arbitrary set of rules and expectations, to follow the parents' patterns for doing whatever the parents desire.

(See chapter 11 for further discussion of the difference between the two styles.)

Punishment by commanding parents is often harsh, and is seldom based on clear expectations or firm boundaries that provide healthy and acceptable choices. The kind of "discipline" used distorts the child's development of self-discipline based on principle and a clear knowledge of right and wrong. Healthy discipline corrects. Harsh punishment, administered by commanding parents, creates more hostility.

There is a more subtle type of "commander-in-chief" parent. Some of these parents make demands more politely; they attempt to appear "open" in their attitudes. But these "low-key" commander parents also try to set their children straight by questioning, analyzing, diagnosing, and handing out prescriptions or punishment.

We've looked at four distinct parenting styles. Each of us will at times discover something of each of these styles within us. Now, we turn to the model after which we can pattern ourselves, as we reject the negative tendencies and trust in God for his supernatural help.

ENCOURAGING PARENTS

Encouraging parents are creative and positive parents who take their model after God's love, care, and discipline. Theirs is a balanced parenting style with room for constructive confrontation, tender comfort and protection, and the control of disciplined living.

The encouraging parenting style is growth-oriented rather than perfectionistic in nature. It is characterized by open communication, listening, sharing, mutual respect and equalization of power, self-respect, a logical and rational approach, empathy, clearly established limits, and firm but loving discipline.

Encouraging parents are responsible parents. Ephesians 6:4 clarifies parental responsibilities: "nurturing and admonishing." Or, paraphrased from the root words: "teaching and discipline, encouragement and correction."

Encouraging parents are communicators. Communication approaches vary with the individual child's emotional needs. Parents must discern when to be supportive, firm, kind, flexible, restrictive, confrontive, helpful, or authoritative.

Encouraging parents are teachers. And often they find themselves tangling with the other "teachers" in our pluralistic society, which thrusts its secular values and attitudes on children. The teaching role is also a correcting role—the kind of correction that encourages right responses rather than breeding discouragement.

While other parenting styles are satisfied with making a point, setting things straight verbally, or making certain that parental expectations are adhered to one way or another, the encouraging style of parenting aims at producing responsible children who have self-discipline and are motivaed internally to make the right choices. The goal of the encouraging parent is to set limits and guidelines so children can make decisions and learn from the natural consequences of living, and to help children learn to choose behavior which is in the best interest of others as well as in their own best interests.

Finally, encouraging parents are learners. The encouraging parent learns to understand who he is, what God wants him to be, and how he can change past patterns of discouraging parenting into positive ones. This learning process takes time and effort, and dependence on our divine Model for his help and guidance. I reflect on my own attempts to learn . . .

Sitting at my desk at home I began penciling my thoughts about God as our model for being parents. "God is our Heavenly Father," I wrote. "He is accessible and approachable. He doesn't always gratify every demand or need, but he doesn't shove us away in anger, either."

Suddenly my thoughts were interrupted. Our five-year-old Jennifer stood quietly at my side, wearing her usual "come play with me" smile. She knew that I was busy, but she felt alone in the house.

Inwardly I was hesitant, because I wanted to meet her need

and get my work completed too. I told myself, "Parents have rights too. We can't let children's wants determine our schedules all the time." But when I looked at Jennifer, I could sense her genuine feeling of loneliness and need for attention. She had been playing by herself for almost two hours while my wife was shopping. Now she wanted her Dad.

Knowing when to take the time to build relationships with children and when to keep on schedule is often a hard decision. Then it struck me. On the front of Jenni's shirt was a picture of a little girl picking flowers with the words written across the bottom, "Take time to smell the flowers." Jenni had worn the outfit many times before, but that moment I understood its meaning for me.

I was glad that I stopped for thirty minutes to spend some time with Jenni. My interruption gave me an opportunity to do something special with my daughter.

Changing parenting styles takes time . . . and parenting takes time. We struggle as we seek to balance our parenting styles. But each new day brings new motivation as we realistically seek to learn what it means to be an encouraging parent. With God's help, we and our children will be on the road to becoming responsible, encouraged, mature human beings.

3 | *When I Grow Up*
I Want to Be a Person

**DEVELOPING A
BLUEPRINT FOR
REACHING FULL
POTENTIAL**

Children are in a constant process of change. In fact, growth and change are the essence of child life. As Frances L. Ilg and Louise Bates Ames state in their book, *Child Behavior,*

> Each and every part of the child's nature has to grow—his sense of self, his fears, his affections and his curiosities; his feelings toward mother and father, brothers and sisters and playmates; his attitudes toward sex; his judgments of good and bad, of ugly and beautiful; his respect for truth and justice; his sense of humor; his ideas about life and death, violence, nature, and deity.[1]

Every child is a unique individual of God's making, and no one individual will react or grow in quite the same way as another. But each child passes through essentially the same growth patterns, at his own speed and with his own special needs and abilities. This is true of physical growth—and also of personality development. Within certain limits we can isolate those factors that contribute to the development of a healthy personality; we can describe the process of healthy growth and pinpoint certain needs that must be met if a child is to reach his full human and spiritual potential. In this chapter we want to develop a blueprint for understanding more about the basic needs and growth patterns of children.

As we look at children's needs and growth processes, it is important that we keep in mind that a child doesn't think like an adult. Children perceive, associate, and interpret their experiences according to the limits of their past experiences and understanding. Their thinking is related to their mental and emotional capacities, and their behavior is based upon their personal perceptions, which may or may not be correct or "logical." They have needs they want satisfied and self-interests they want to protect, and they behave in ways that seem to them appropriate to getting those needs met and those interests protected. In other words, the world looks different from a child's point of view, and to help our children we need to make an effort to understand their natures, their needs, and their feelings about life. Children are whole persons with complex needs, wants, fears, desires, and questions. We must keep this in mind if we want to help our children grow toward their full potential physically, mentally, emotionally, and spiritually.

PERSONALITY DEVELOPMENT AND PERSONAL GROWTH

The first section of our blueprint for reaching full potential is summarized by figure 3-1 on page 33. This diagram is designed to help us understand what factors shape a child's personality, and how these factors relate to the process of healthy growth. But we parents are growing too; these factors and processes also apply to us! By examining the way our children grow, we can gain insight into our own

Figure 3-1
Personality Formation and
the Process of Growth

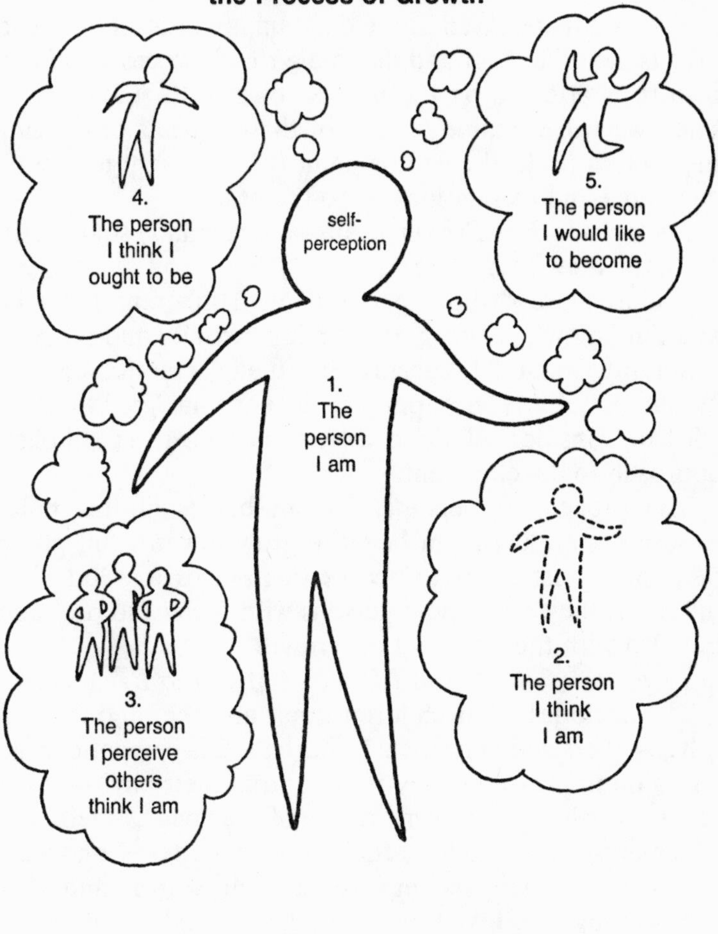

4.
The person
I think I
ought to be

self-
perception

5.
The person
I would like
to become

1.
The
person
I am

3.
The person
I perceive
others
think I am

2.
The person
I think
I am

THE PROCESS OF HEALTHY GROWTH

1. Accept ourselves as God views us—as we are.
2. Be open to our faults while accepting ourselves realistically.
3. Be open to feedback from other people.
4. Begin to reject unrealistic goals and self-expectations.
5. Begin to set realistic goals.

growth needs, and we can understand more fully the
process of becoming the mature, responsible parents we
want to be.

The factors pictured in the diagram are interrelated; each
affects the other four and the total growth process, and each
in turn is affected by the process of growth. Later in this
book we will examine several of these aspects of development in more detail. At this point I simply want to identify
each area and its relationship to the others:

Factor #1: The Person I Am—body, mind, soul, spirit,
and how they interrelate.

Children are "whole persons" with inherent resources
and limitations, growing to their full capacity and potential
physically, mentally, socially, spiritually, emotionally, and
psychologically. (The approach to personal growth which
tries to consider all these aspects is known as a holistic
approach to development.)

The process of personal growth begins at this point.
Before our children can begin to grow towards full potential, they must learn to accept themselves as God views
them—as they are, whole persons with faults and problems
but also with the potential for growth.

Factor #2: The Person I Perceive Myself to Be.

This includes what children think and feel about themselves—their self-concepts. Children's self-perceptions are
based on impressions they receive from their environment,
other people, their own styles of behavior, their self-
statements, their bodies, their growth patterns and visu-
alized goals, their feelings about their worth, and their
needs to love, be loved, belong, achieve, and be fulfilled or
satisfied. Children grow when their self-perceptions are
realistic but positive, when they are open to their faults and
can respond to them and avoid overreacting with hurt and
defensiveness.

Self-perception is probably the most important aspect of
personality formation, as it affects and results from all other
aspects. How children learn to perceive themselves deter-

mines to a large extent the kind of persons they will become.

Factor #3: The Person I Perceive Others Think I Am.

What other people say and do to children influences what they think and feel about who they are. Other people can shape a child's thinking and feeling processes both positively and negatively. The family system is especially important to development. How a family communicates and relates greatly influences what kind of people the children in that family will become.

Growing to full potential means being open to feedback from others without overreacting to their expectations. Children grow when they learn to reach out to others and to develop more meaningful relationships by improving communication skills and by focusing on the positive in relationships. By learning to take responsibility for their own actions, they avoid blame, overdependence, and other relationship-warping attitudes.

Factor #4: The Person I Think I Ought, Should, or Must Become in Order to Be Loved and Accepted, to Feel I Belong, to Achieve, to Feel Satisfied and Fulfilled.

These are the self-defeating demands, wishes, or expectations children pick up from others and keep for themselves. This could be called a "neurotic guilt or conflict zone" of personality development; it is what Karen Horney has called "the tyranny of the shoulds."[2]

Unrealistic, unattainable, discouraging self-demands prevent children from learning the skills they need for overcoming conflict, circumstances, problems, or personal limitations, and diminish their ability to accept themselves and learn from past failures. Real growth means beginning to reject these negative and unachievable goals in favor of more realistic, less legalistic ones.

Factor #5: The Person I Would Like to Become.

This is the model person or ideal self that is the proper goal of the growth process—the person children visualize themselves becoming as they acquire the necessary skills of self-understanding, self-acceptance, and self-actualization. This is a realistic goal based on their value system and their understanding of God's Word; it includes ideas, beliefs, morals, and accepted limitations, and it is shaped and guided by the teaching and modeling they receive at home. For our purposes, this model would be an encouraged, positive, responsible, maturing human being. We help children grow toward becoming their ideal selves as we set realistic goals that further enable them to reach their full potential, using the principles outlined in this book and the principles found in Scripture.

NEEDS AND THE GROWTH PROCESS

As we stated at the beginning of the chapter, the process of growth is natural and necessary for children. The same is true for parents; we were designed to strive toward becoming more mature, responsible people. But we all have certain needs which must be met if we are to grow. Healthy personality development and self-esteem are influenced by the way the family and society meet or fail to meet those needs.

The second part of our "blueprint" for growth and development is based on the concepts of the psychologist Abraham Maslow, who described what he believed was the necessary process by which one could become a responsible and fulfilled person. No theory is completely applicable to our approach—I shall be adapting some of Maslow's ideas to relate specifically to parenting and child development—but Maslow's study provides us with a logical outline for understanding the relationship between needs and personal growth.

Maslow's view of human development focuses on the positive inherent potentials of a person to grow towards a goal. (This would correspond to "The Person I Would Like to Become" in the chart on p. 33.) Maslow described this process as being like an acorn which seems to strive toward becoming an oak tree. This tendency toward self-realization is termed "self-actualization."

But Maslow held that when certain basic needs are not adequately met in a developing child or adult, that person will sacrifice his ultimate goals and potentials to satisfy the more demanding immediate need. Maslow posited a "hierarchy of needs" in which the basic "animal needs" of survival progress to "higher" human and spiritual needs. Maslow's outline can be depicted as a pyramid, shown in figure 3-2.

Figure 3-2
Maslow's Hierarchy of Needs

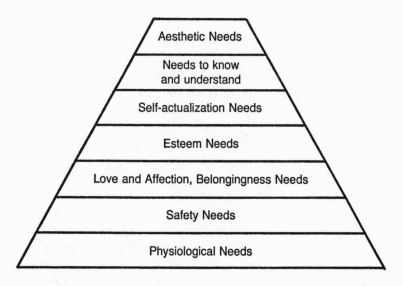

Briefly, I want to identify each of the areas of need in Maslow's hierarchy and relate them to parenting and child development:[3]

Physiological Needs. A child's first cluster of needs is physical—for food, rest, oxygen, thirst satisfaction, touch, comfort, warmth, elimination, and so on. Throughout each stage of a child's life, parents must discover how to adequately and appropriately meet his physical needs and

must ultimately teach the child to care for his own physiological necessities. (Sex education, by the way, begins in
early childhood with the attitudes and actions communicated within the family.)

Our physical states greatly affect how we act and feel.
When a child is tired, cross, hungry, or in physical pain, our
methods of discipline and our expectations must differ from
those we use in other circumstances. Likewise, the physical
condition of parents affects the way they treat their children. Acknowledging and meeting physical needs are important first steps in fostering healthy growth.

Safety or Security Needs. The second constellation of
needs relates to physical and psychological safety, shelter,
economic provision, emotional surety, trust, predictability,
the avoidance of pain, fear, and hurt. I would include at this
level the need for personal acceptance. Children need
reassurance of personal safety and inner security before
they can grow. They must feel a sense of acceptance within
their family. Rejection, unnecessary fear, emotional pain,
or mistrust can severely hinder the development of self-
confidence and self-acceptance. Constant criticism causes
withdrawal from possible failure or rejection, and causes
children to feel that they must constantly protect themselves. This inhibits personal growth.

This second set of needs in Maslow's hierarchy is actually
the first set of needs in our psychological blueprint, and the
first step in healthy personal growth. Before a child can
grow toward "maturity" or "self-actualization," he must
have the security of feeling he is accepted and cared for as
he is.

Love and Affection, and Belongingness Needs. Here I
depart slightly from Maslow's outline. In this book I have
fully explained these needs in the chapter on self-esteem
(chapter 4) under two categories—the need "to be significant or loved" and the need "to belong." Families are
important first sources of filling these needs. The chapters
on evaluating family atmosphere and on developing effec-

tive communication (chapters 1 and 6) can also provide insight into how families can best provide for these needs.

Esteem Needs. We all have the need for self-respect, for the esteem and respect of others, for status, prestige, recognition, importance, approval, for the independence of personality that leads to feelings of self-confidence, adequacy, usefulness, and worth. Having these needs met is absolutely crucial to the development of a healthy personality. Chapter 4 explains in detail how self-esteem is developed and fostered in families.

Self-Actualization Needs. Self-actualization needs in Maslow's outline include the needs for creativity and self-expression, for realizing one's highest potential, for mature relationships with others, for religious and artistic expression and for feelings of growth.

In our emphasis this would include the need to become loving, responsible, communicating persons in every stage of life. For parents, it involves becoming encouraging, responsible parents as described in chapter 1 and illustrated throughout this book. "Self-actualization" also relates to the concept of the "image of God" within us as our model for growth towards maturity and fulfillment, and to our "model person," our goal for growth in personality development.

The Needs to Know and Understand. Maslow described these needs as the desire and ability to explore, discover, and integrate all truth into daily life and into the world in which we live. For us it also relates to the need for assurance and guidance from God's Word as it provides meaning and purpose to our lives.

Aesthetic Needs. Maslow included in this "highest" group of needs the need for beauty, symmetry, order, harmony, perfection of structure, ecstasy, and mystic experience. For our purposes, "Aesthetic Needs" would probably most closely relate to a Christian's need for prayerful communion with God. This would be an expression of faith, worship, and praise, and would result in spiritual growth.

ANOTHER NEED

There is another strategic need which is lacking in Maslow's approach and in most approaches to child training and human development. It could be labeled the "redemptive need."

Human nature is supremely self-centered. We and our children have the "need" to become less self-centered and more God-centered and other-centered. In Matthew 22:37–40, Jesus summarized in two commandments the principles for godly living: "Love the Lord your God with all your heart, soul, and mind, . . . and love your neighbor as you love yourself."

At the root of all mankind's wrong behavior is self-worship. Human nature is predisposed toward sin and selfishness. We have the capacity to sin and a tendency toward sinning as well as the potential for growth. It's easy for us to put ourselves in the place of God and make our choices on the basis of what pleases or fulfills our selfish needs rather than what is right or best.

But our needs as humans can never be fully met unless we are rightly related to God, to ourselves, and to others. People who center their lives in themselves cannot reach total fulfillment; they are not functioning as they were designed. Because we are made in the image of God, we can never escape the need to be forgiven and restored to a loving and worshipful relationship with our God through Jesus Christ.

This is more than adding a religious system to life. We are dealing with the basic problems of man's nature. In speaking of a "redemptive need," we're speaking of the need for a supernatural and radical internal change which deals with our self-centeredness and restores the "Image of God" in us. It gives us new capacity and power to gain freedom from our egocentricity and to become more fulfilled and fully functioning persons.

DESIGNED TO BE DEPENDENT

We are of great worth to God. He would have us respond to his love and plan for our lives and for our families. God designed us to be dependent upon him and to trust him by living in loving obedience—our greatest need is for him. When we confess our sins, rest in his forgiveness, and grow in our relationship with him, we are functioning as children of God, as members of his family. Then he gives us new capacities and new motivations toward living responsibly. This is his intention for us, and we never reach our full potential until this need is fulfilled.

DESIGNED TO GROW

In summary, we've seen that each child (and every parent, too!) is a total person, designed to grow and develop in every aspect of his or her being. Every part of his or her nature interacts powerfully on every other part. How children view themselves and feel about themselves—their self-concept—is crucial to how they will develop, although their thinking is limited by their perspective and experience and their perception and thinking patterns change as they grow. Every child has certain basic physical and psychological needs, and how these needs are met is important to his overall development. Among these needs, and just as important as the needs commonly discussed by psychologists and students of child development, is the need for a personal encounter and relationship with a loving God. And included is the spiritual need to find ultimate meaning and purpose in the person of God's Son. Jesus promised that as "the way, the truth, and the life" he had come "that all might have life . . . more abundantly." We are of great worth to him, and he is essential to our well-being. When our spiritual needs are met, we have a greater capacity and potential to fulfill our total needs.

4 | *Self Esteem: The Bottom-Line Issue*

HELPING CHILDREN DEVELOP HEALTHY SELF-ESTEEM

Years ago, my child psychology professor, James Hatch, told of an incident that occurred shortly after his fourth son was born. One day, as his wife was putting their newborn to bed, their five-year-old peered over the bassinet observing his brother. He pondered. Then, after a few moments, he looked up at his mother and queried, "Mom, *does he know who he is* . . . or does he just lie there and think that he's nobody?"

He was close to voicing a profound truth. We do indeed become the persons we think and feel we are. The writer of Proverbs puts the same truth pointedly: "As a person thinks within himself, so is he" (Prov. 23:7). The extent to which we value ourselves—our self-esteem—affects:

—how we manage our personal survival to meet our own
needs,
—how responsible we feel for meeting others' needs,
—how able we are to develop closeness and intimacy with
others,
—how we handle conflict and solve problems,
—how productive and successful we become,
—how we search for meaning and purpose in life,
—how we use our own resources for coping with life, and
—how we communicate and relate with others.

Healthy self-esteem is a realistic appraisal of one's worth
which begets a confident, joyful feeling of security. Unlike
self-centeredness or conceit, it doesn't have the need to put
down others in order to build up self. Self-esteem is a
relaxed self-view, based on a feeling of personal legitimacy.
"I'm acceptable" is the bottom-line emotion.

A healthy self-esteem is essential to healthy emotional
and spiritual growth. If we feel good about ourselves, we
will become productive, confident, effective communicators
who enjoy relating to people. Low self-esteem eventually
surfaces as depression, anxiety, guilt, and other patterns of
withdrawal. Concisely, the symptoms of low self-esteem can
be contrasted with healthy self-esteem:

Low Feelings of Worth	Healthy Feelings of Worth
Manipulates self and others—strives for control	Accepts self and others as worthwhile people
Depends on "wants" to be happy—selfish	Aware of others, respects them
Deceitful, phoney, wears "masks"—mistrustful	Trusting, creative, spontaneous
Tries to please, and expects to be placated	Accepts personal responsibility

Aggressive, demanding, and hurtful, perhaps subtly	Assertive and truthful with the kind of caring confrontation that builds relationships
Closed, defensive, bored	Open, objective, interested

Self-respect, self-acceptance, and self-confidence are the building blocks for living. One of the greatest gifts an encouraging parent can give a child is a healthy self-view.

HEALTHY SELF-ESTEEM BEGINS IN CHILDHOOD

How others relate to us affects our self-image. And the kinds of relationships and communications we experience early in life are especially important to the way we view ourselves; they continue to influence how we relate with others throughout life. Inside each of us is a "tape recording" of early messages which can either discourage or encourage us. We develop and internalize these "scripts" (as some psychologists refer to them) according to the way other people communicate and act toward us. These become a part of our belief systems and behavior patterns. We can "rescript" ourselves according to our model of who we want to be, and we are continually in the process of becoming, growing, and changing, but we will continue to carry with us the influence of many of those early memories and feelings.

Our internalized self-perception—our life "script"—becomes the mental and emotional blueprint for the way we think, feel, and behave, the basis for how we adapt and adjust to life situations. Individuals who develop poor self-images during childhood often become restless, depressed, unhappy adults—anxious, boxed-in, unable to focus on their creative potential.

June stared down at the floor. She was a bright, attractive, caring person, but she was obsessed with feelings of having been mistreated and short-changed in life. Her hurt ran deep:

It's the hell of being torn by the realization that nobody really loves me. I feel so rejected. I feel totally unacceptable and incompetent at everything I try to do. The more I try to change, the more I fail. . . .

Sometimes I feel like I'm intelligent and even creative inside. Those thoughts are pushed out when I remember what my parents kept telling me. I used to rebel because I thought they were just sarcastic putdowns, but *perhaps my parents were right*. The more I fight, the more those memories haunt me.

I hate myself because I blame my parents, and then feel so guilty. Sometimes I hate them so intensely, but they are my parents and I want them to love me so much. I want them to love me for who I am so badly I could scream. The longer I live the less I get done, and I don't feel worth anything unless I can get something done. At times I want to kill myself, but I can't because I'm afraid death will be too much like the hell I'm carrying around in my head now. My Christian friends tell me to let go and let God give me peace. They just don't know the pain. I'm so confused. I want to be loved physically, but sex seems so dirty. It's too painful anymore to be accepted by anyone. My friends keep telling me how I should feel if I am a Christian. Perhaps I'm not really a Christian at all . . .

June is an extreme example of the chronic loneliness and depression that can result from negative childhood experiences. Children who grow up in negative environments fail to feel accepted for who they are; they feel accepted only when they achieve, and generally they feel incapable of meeting parental expectations. They fail to gain a sense of identity through belonging and to develop the social skills necessary for acquiring satisfying close relationships. The fear of being hurt and rejected again makes them closed and defensive. They feel aimless and alienated, and keep searching for some purpose in life.

June ached with pain, and longed for encouragement in the midst of her depression. Extreme cases such as hers illustrate the tragic results of a crushed spirit, a self-concept downtrodden by the lack of encouragement in the developmental years. People such as June can be helped, although the healing process is often complex and gradual. But how much better if the pain of a negative self-concept can be avoided, if a child can be given a healthy self-esteem early in life!

COMPONENTS OF HEALTHY SELF-ESTEEM

There are four basic needs which must be met if a person is to develop self-esteem, and four corresponding components of healthy self-esteem; they are listed in table 4-1. Here is a brief description of each:

Table 4-1
Components of Healthy Self-Esteem

THE NEED	MET BY BEING	MAKES US FEEL	WHICH RESULTS IN
To be significant	Affirmed	Worthwhile or loved	Self-respect
To belong	Involved	Recognized or appreciated	Self-acceptance
To achieve	Acknowledged	Competent or successful	Self-confidence
To be satisfied	Contented	Pleasure or happy	Self-fulfillment

Significance-Respect. The first need is to feel worthwhile and loved for who we are—the need to be significant. We all value ourselves to the degree that we perceive we are valued by others.

Children especially have this need to be affirmed and respected as individuals. In his book, *Why Am I Afraid to Tell You Who I Am?,* John Powell shares a conversation he had with a friend, who said, "I am afraid to tell you who I

am because . . . you may not like who I am, and it's all that
I have."[1] Children feel this way sometimes. We must assure
our children they are loved and accepted as the individuals
they are, for they have nothing else to offer us. If we
encourage our children by affirming them as significant
persons, we encourage the development of their self-
respect.

Belongingness-Acceptance. The second need of self-identity is the need to belong, to overcome natural feelings of
inferiority, loneliness, and rejection. We need to feel
involved and important—unique and needed in our families, jobs, and churches. One of God's primary reasons for
instituting the family must have been to provide a basic
sense of belonging for every human being. An early sense of
belonging provides the security base of being recognized
and appreciated, and equips a child for weathering the
storms of interpersonal relationships.

We learn to accept others as we have been accepted. One
of the tremendous benefits of being a Christian is knowing
we have been unconditionally accepted in Christ. Through
faith in Jesus Christ, we have total acceptance into God's
family. The unconditional love and acceptance of God when
we come to him in repentance is constant, not based on our
worthiness or "goodness." The fact that God loves us when
we are so unlovely should encourage us to accept ourselves
as he accepts us—and in turn to accept one another.

The "belonging" for which we all deeply yearn is found
most completely in God's loving recognition. But children
first learn this lovely feeling of unconditional belonging in
their homes. If we are encouraging parents, involving our
children in meaningful conversations and activities, then
they will feel appreciated. When we demonstrate recognition to them, they will sense that they belong, and we will
be encouraging the development of self-acceptance.

Achievement-Confidence. The third need of self-identity
is the need to achieve, to make progress toward success.
Children need to be encouraged toward being personally
responsible, especially in assuming the consequences for
what they do. But it needs to be stressed that not only is

there a sense of enjoyment in completing a task, but the process itself lends a sense of competence. They need to know that the efforts we make toward our goals are as important as the achievements themselves. For children who learn a healthy attitude toward achievement, failure in any particular endeavor is not total defeat, and the fear of failure becomes less of a threat because of the benefit that can be found in learning from mistakes along the way. Rewards become more intrinsic—they prove to themselves that they can be productive and creative in their accomplishments.

Honest, positive, and appropriate acknowledgment encourages children to feel good about themselves and increases their confidence in being able to achieve new tasks. It helps them move from inertia and fear to a learned ability to face new challenges and to handle their own problems. As children gain *competence* in doing something they consider worthwhile and receive recognition and encouragement for it, *self-confidence* will be internalized.

The need to achieve is not healthy when it dominates personality obsessively. The person who is rejected by his peers because of inadequacies may focus his attention on tasks instead of people. Instead of developing a healthy feeling of self-worth in a network of accepting relationships, he tries to gain acceptance by what can be achieved.

The result is further isolation and loneliness, for this kind of behavior is inevitably competitive, and the self-esteem it produces inevitably short-lived. The task-centered person plays a serious game of "oneupmanship," and he finds it increasingly difficult to trust others. He is more likely to see others as objects to be manipulated and ultimately defeated. His past achievements come to seem empty to him, and he is terrified of failing.

The sense of realistic achievement—healthy, encouraged, and acknowledged—is quite different. The resulting self-confidence is neither cocky nor offensive.

Satisfaction-Fulfillment. The fourth self-identity need is the need to be satisfied, to find personal fulfillment. This fourth need actually summarizes the first three needs mentioned, in that self-esteem is essentially the self-fulfillment gained from feeling significant and loved, from having a sense of belonging, and from having accomplished something worthwhile.

Satisfaction is often elusive in our culture. We measure fulfillment by the degree to which we are able to gratify our needs and desires. Yet it is possible to maximize the pleasures and minimize the drudgery of life, to strive for peace of mind and body, and still face the end of our lives in disappointment.

One reason for this is that our perceptions of life have become distorted. Popular songs convey much of contemporary thought on the search for true happiness and personal fulfillment. Such lines as "I can't smile without you, can't live without you"; "It can't be wrong when it feels so right"; and "I know I need to be in love" indicate certain fallacies in our belief systems. Those lines tell us that, in order to be happy, we must do what feels good to us, and that what feels good is right, and that we can't be fulfilled unless our insatiable needs are being met. Since we can't always feel happy, or have everything we want, we are never satisfied.

The overemphasis on competition and overachievement is another example of our culture's distorted view of self-fulfillment. We may be temporarily admired for our status, wealth, beauty, intelligence, power, or charisma. We may even be deceived into admiring ourselves for these marks of "success," but we will probably be bothered with uncomfortable feelings of inferiority as we struggle to maintain our "image."

True fulfillment comes with a recognition and acceptance of the *truth* in our deepest selves. That truth is the revelation of ourselves in light of who God is and what he desires for us. It is finding true satisfaction within ourselves as we understand God's provisions for us as taught in Scripture: "Ye shall know the truth, and the truth shall set you free."

The Bible is not a tranquilizer which blunts the impact of facing reality. But God does give us the challenge of personal integrity and then provides the moral guidelines and standards for living toward his Best. God's peace grows within us as we discern through Scripture how to deal with the inevitable conflicts that threaten to destroy peace. We begin to understand that God has purpose in history, and that, as his children, we derive our ultimate satisfaction from him.

The Christian begins with truth about himself and his world and then he is free to pursue goals which allow him to develop his character and confidence. Fulfillment is a by-product, not a goal. The responsible parent tries to help his children develop a positive self-esteem; he attempts to provide an encouraging environment to nurture the development of self-respect, self-acceptance, self-confidence, and self-fulfillment. But such a goal can only be fully accomplished as we introduce our children to the truth about themselves, God, and his designs for us.

COUNTERFEIT SELF-ESTEEM

As with everything, Satan has his counterfeit for healthy self-worth. If self-esteem isn't developed through growth in integrity, honesty, and love, a counterfeit self-esteem, based on self-centered sensuality and greed, can take over. Table 4-2 contrasts different self-views.

Table 4-2
Views of Self

FEELING	BELIEF	ATTITUDE	BEHAVIOR
Healthy self-esteem	Realistic view of self	"I'm equal in worth to others"	Acceptable
Pride or self-centered-ness	Unrealistic comparison of self	"I'm better than others"	Obnoxious
Low self-esteem	Unworthy feelings	"I'm worse than others"	Defensive

Children and adults have built-in motivators for self-preservation which can produce self-centeredness. The drive toward self-preservation was meant to be the motivation for developing full creative potential in life—not selfishness. Self-centeredness, rooted in our sinful human natures, leads to pride—a cocky, unrealistic attitude which blames, ridicules, and rationalizes in order to achieve a sense of purpose in life. A self-centered personality values only one's own inflated and unrealistic sense of worth. It assumes a position of superiority rather than mutual respect or equality.

Numerous books written today confuse or blend self-centeredness with healthy self-esteem. Knowing the difference is essential to building feelings of worth in ourselves and in our children.

UNDERSTANDING BUILDS SELF-ESTEEM

As children hear parents speak about them, they begin to form their concept of themselves. Dr. Craig W. Ellison relates:

> Parents communicate acceptance or rejection in many ways by whether they meet [the child's] needs without lengthy delays; by the way in which the child is held, caressed, and talked to; by the frequency and form of discipline; by the amount of spontaneous affection they show; by how much they interact with the child.
>
> Parental rejection may destroy the attachment bond if extreme, but more often it handicaps the child by damaging his self-esteem. When the child receives mostly negative responses from the people who are most significant in his life, a foundation of doubt and insecurity is laid. The child who feels rejected by his parents is likely to conclude that he's not good enough to be wanted by anybody. He is afraid to approach others for fear of further rejection. Persons with low self-esteem are less open in relating to others than are people with normal self-esteem, and they are more likely to have their feelings hurt. Furthermore, they feel too "weak" to overcome their problems. Either they assume that nobody would want

anything to do with them because they don't have anything to offer, or they behave in ways that tend to repel others. Rejection by parents also hinders people from forming the basic trust that is essential to an intimate relationship.[2]

Parents' attitudes and moods have powerful effects on children. Their communication either conveys respect and acceptance or disappointment and disinterest. Healthy self-esteem is nurtured when we take the appropriate time to relate with our children spiritually, socially, emotionally, physically—all at a sharing and caring level.

"Daddy, I don't know what's wrong with me," our five-year-old Jennifer cried as I was putting her to bed one evening. We had already been through a thirty-minute "No, I don't want to go to bed" routine. And I didn't know what to do.

Sometimes children test parents by seeking attention or pity. At other times they are genuinely crying out for understanding and reassurance that they are "OK." The process of learning to ignore their attention-getting devices and yet being sure to affirm them as persons takes time, wisdom, and patience. Some parents can quickly discern which response to make, but I've been the kind who has had to wrestle with most situations until I discovered the appropriate solution.

"I'm hungry," Jenni cried again. We had figured out that Jenni would often confuse "hungry" with the feelings of being tired and frustrated. Children (and adults!) sometimes mix their physical and emotional needs when they are weary. Hunger wasn't Jenni's problem that night. She was confused and physically exhausted.

Jenni continued to plead, "Daddy, I don't know what's wrong with me." I paused, reflected for a moment, and responded. "I know, honey; sometimes we just feel all mixed up and hurt inside. I understand and I love you." She began to quiet down and replied, "Daddy, I love you, too." Within minutes she fell asleep.

Jenni needed to go to bed because she was tired and required rest. Yet she didn't want to be alone because she needed the nearness of someone she loved and the reassurance that she was loved and accepted. She felt that something was wrong with her and she didn't like feeling that way. She needed to know that she was "OK," that it was acceptable and normal to feel confused, and that her inner feelings and thoughts were affirmed and valid. And she *was* affirmed, because someone special to her really cared for her and her feelings.

We as parents have tremendous influence on our children's self-esteem. Our attitudes and emotions toward our children—revealed by our actions, facial expressions, and tone of voice as well as by the ideas and values we express verbally—become mirrors which reflect to the child who he is. If we communicate an attitude of superiority or disrespect towards our children, they will feel misunderstood and inferior. If we communicate a belief that they can't succeed at a difficult task, they will begin to doubt their abilities.

But when we believe in our children and communicate that we value them for who they are, they react positively. When we listen, show understanding, and express genuine concern, they respond warmly. They begin to value themselves and have confidence in their abilities. As they begin to know themselves, understand themselves, believe in and love themselves, they learn how to know, understand, accept, trust, and love others.

Self-esteem is God's gift to the Christian who finds his or her spiritual identity in Christ Jesus. We parents, in his grace, can be his instruments for developing this gift, the sense of self-worth, in our children. The more healthy our children's self-esteem, the more potential they will have to develop character and responsibility. The more responsible we are as parents, the more we will find our fulfillment in encouraging our children's self-worth.

PARENTS ARE PEOPLE, TOO

As we consider helping our children develop healthy self-views, it is important not to ignore our own needs for growth and development. Parents need healthy self-concepts, too. It is *essential* that we feel good about ourselves as parents, marriage partners, and persons if we are to help our children develop positive self-views.

Discouraged parents can lash out at their children and create confusion. Parents who are struggling with their own negative self-concepts and internalized anger can create a home environment of hurt and rejection. Encouraged parents, on the other hand, are likely to have the inner resources to be encouraging to their children. They will have the ability to create positive home environments characterized by warmth and acceptance.

The most refreshing way we can deal with our own needs and problems is to openly admit that we don't have all the answers, that we are people in the process of coping with changes in our lives. Our children are keen observers of our fallibilities. When they see that we try to deal honestly with our own problems, but that we also desire to grow to our greatest potential, they are assured that they can trust us. And as we understand our own difficulties and build our own sense of self-worth, they will be given a valuable model. Our example will be an inheritance which they can treasure throughout life.

5 | *Sometimes I Feel So Discouraged*

CULTIVATING THE ART OF ENCOURAGEMENT

"Will you please explain to me why I feel the way I do?"
"I don't understand why I feel so useless. Nothing matters any more."
"I'm not happy and I don't like myself."

Every week I hear comments like these from discouraged people who long for hope and affirmation. All of us experience discouragement at times. But for many whose childhood memories are characterized by discouragement, despair can become a way of life.

Discouragement goes hand in hand with low self-esteem. When we feel worthless or hopeless our attitude on life suffers:

The California Indians have a saying, 'In the beginning God gave everyone a cup from which to drink. Our cup is broken.' It

is almost impossible to drink from a broken cup. It is just as
difficult to be up when your self-esteem is down.[1]

We as parents hold the keys to our children's self-esteem.
If we want our children to develop into happy, responsible
adults, it is up to us to see that their "cups" don't get
broken. By developing the art of encouragement, we can
help them build healthy attitudes which will motivate them
throughout their lives.

Encouragement focuses on the assets and strengths of our
children, giving them the confidence that comes from
feeling appreciated. Encouraging children helps them value
themselves, believe in their abilities, and benefit from their
mistakes.

That is what we want for our children. But our good
intentions are sometimes thwarted by our failure to help
them believe and feel that they are acceptable for who they
are, not just for the things about them that please us. We
can turn our good intentions into specific encouraging
experiences by developing positive attitudes and objectives.
In this chapter I want to explore seven objectives that will
prove helpful in cultivating an encouraging parenting style.

*Objective #1: Accepting Ourselves and Our Children As
We Are.*

Learning to accept ourselves and our children as we are,
with all our imperfections, is necessary to helping them
develop a sense of self-worth. Acceptance encourages.
Nonacceptance discourages. Parental acceptance cannot be
based on a child's performance.

It is possible to reject misbehavior without rejecting a
child's honest feelings. We can reject unacceptable attitudes
without breaking the child's spirit. A child needs loving,
helpful encouragement to fulfill the expectations parents
rapidly hurl at him. Constant faultfinding, blaming, humili-
ating, nagging, and lecturing only cause discouragement.

An example recently expressed to me was:

> When I was a child and teenager I used to struggle with my
> feelings. Whenever I expressed something with which Dad

would disagree he would snap back, *'No, you don't feel that way!'* I wish he could have just listened to me and helped me understand how to change. Instead, I grew up always thinking I had to be somebody other than who I was. Neither I nor my feelings were accepted.

Children sometimes irritate and embarrass us, and we overreact in pride or self-defense. It is easy to find fault in our children, to put them down or humiliate them when we feel that our status or self-image is threatened. When that happens, we need to apologize, to admit that we made a mistake. When we accept our own imperfections and allow for slip-ups, we give our children an example they will want to emulate.

Objective #2: Avoiding Double Standards.

Double standards in the family won't work. We can't tell the children to keep their rooms in order and expect them to comply when we carelessly scatter our clothes around the house. If Dad complains that he is tired from working and decides to let the lawn go another few days, yet insists that his children complete their chores, then the children become resentful.

It is inconsistent for us as parents to "talk down" to children and then turn around and punish them for talking back or showing disrespect to us. When we occasionally lose self-control and explode verbally, but get insulted if our children sometimes express their frustration and anger— there is a double standard. If we expect to be excused for being human, we need to be tolerant toward our children and understand their shortcomings.

If our children are disrespectful, perhaps we need to examine our own attitudes and examples. They may be responding to our inconsistency; we may be breaking our own rules. But they can be encouraged if we admit our lack of self-control and express an honest desire to change.

One evening my daughter told me, "Daddy, you sure are being grumpy with me tonight." I had an option. I could have snapped, "Don't you dare talk to your father that way!" Or I could have said, "I guess I am, Mary. I've had a very hard day today and I think I'm dumping my frustration on you."

In this instance, I owned up to my feelings, and Mary in turn owned up to hers. She replied, "Sorry you're tired, Daddy; I'll get my things cleaned up. Thanks for telling me that you were tired and not mad at me."

There are times when it is not possible to explain all our reasons for expecting children to obey. The more respect we show them, however, the more they will cooperate when we need them to obey without questioning or arguing.

Objective #3: Recognizing That Guilt Doesn't Motivate.

Attempting to motivate, change, or improve children's behavior by using guilt is self-defeating. A person cannot improve unless he feels good about himself and believes he can change. Constantly reminding children of their faults and failures cannot make them feel better about themselves; harping about their mistakes cannot help them become more responsible. Children need encouragement in order to gain the courage and conviction to change. Creating a sense of shame only discourages.

Dorothy Corkhill Briggs explains:

> Think about yourself for a moment. Don't you behave differently in situations where you feel confident than you do when you feel inadequate? When you're sure of yourself, you make positive statements about yourself. Then, you are friendlier, more outgoing, and interested in becoming peacefully involved with others. When you feel inadequate and bumbling, you shrink from the limelight. The very term, self-confidence, means inner sureness. It says that at the core you trust your capacities, and you act accordingly. So it is with children.[2]

To avoid producing guilt in children, it is helpful to ask ourselves several questions about the way we communicate with them. We can ask ourselves, "Will what I am saying change his behavior? Will it encourage her self-confidence, or will my words hinder her efforts to improve?"

We can also ask, "Am I using guilt as a method of

controlling my children? Am I giving them an example of self-control, or am I trying to make them feel so bad that they will do what I want them to?" Words like "bad," "dirty," "ugly," "shameful," "no good," or "sinful" can be used to control children. But when children hear these words they feel guilty and react negatively:

> We think they will change if we make them feel bad enough. But this is wrong. The Holy Spirit convicts of sin. And we should teach our children [the difference between] right and wrong. But we can do this without making them feel 'no good' or 'useless.' Motivation by guilt causes one of two reactions. Some children behave correctly but develop feelings of depression. Others react to guilt motivations by turning to bad behavior. They think, 'Since my parents think I'm bad, I may as well behave that way!'[3]

Good behavior flows from positive reinforcement and affirmation. Realistic, sincere, genuine compliments support children in their attempts to improve. Motivation by guilt does not.

Incidentally, guilt can be a trap for parents, too. The guilt game affects children when it affects their parents' feelings and relationships. A parent whose disposition is guilt-ridden will certainly feel inadequate, and will have trouble improving his or her parenting style. Guilt peddling between husband and wife threatens marriage stability and sets a bad example. Learning to build each other up instead of tearing each other down is an important step in improving all family relationships.

Objective #4: Separating the Deed from the Doer.

We can improve our efforts to encourage children by learning to "separate the deed from the doer." This also helps to avoid producing guilt. Children will not always perform in the way we expect them to. We can let them know that they are still valued, even though they have disobeyed or failed. And it is very important to help children realize that they can learn from their mistakes.

One day following dinner our daughter, who was then five years old, was excitedly rattling off her day's major events. I had asked, "Tell me about school today." She replied, "Well, today I went outside for recess . . . but I couldn't play 'cause I didn't do something I was 'posed to . . . so I got to sit and watch . . . and I saw a flying worm . . . he was flying around . . . I told Mom and she said she had to do that once too when she was little and that it was OK 'cause that's the way we learn . . ."

My wife and I are not always model parents, but at that moment I had the feeling we were doing something right! Children need to be encouraged to share disappointments and failures and still be assured of love and acceptance. Making it clear to children that they are more important to us than what they do will help them grow up self-confident, responsible, and accepting of others.

Objective #5: Realizing That Comparisons Promote Competition.

We as parents are usually unaware of promoting competition and making unnecessary comparisons in order to motivate a child, but we often do just that. Feelings are easily hurt when one child is affirmed for his efforts or contributions and another is ignored or criticized. This comparison need not be expressed verbally; a child is sensitive to approval or disapproval implied by our facial expression or tone of voice.

Comparisons are made most often on the standards of physical appearance and intelligence. We tend to favor children who do well in school or who are pretty, cute, or good looking. Children become discouraged when parents say, "Why don't you study and make good grades like your brother (or your sister or your friends)." Such comparison tells them they are less appreciated because they don't perform as well as someone else. In his excellent book, *Hide or Seek,* James Dobson summarizes two chapters on beauty and intelligence by saying:

> I have emphasized the critical importance of two factors, beauty and intelligence, in shaping self-esteem and confidence.

For men, physical attractiveness gradually submerges as a value during late adolescence and early adulthood, yielding first place to intelligence. For women, however, beauty retains its number-one position throughout life, even into middle age and beyond. The reason the average woman would rather have beauty than brains is because she knows the average man can see better than he can think. Her value system is based on his and will probably continue that way. A man's physical preferences are also rooted in the opinions of the opposite sex, since most women value intelligence over handsomeness in men.[4]

Comparisons between children are also commonly made in the areas of competitive sports, student activities, academic achievement, and financial and social status. Social ineptitude, physical handicaps, lack of experience and "maturity," or embarrassing family characteristics can be unkindly emphasized by comparisons. Children feel inferior when they are slow learners, unable to speak confidently, unable to make friends easily, or culturally deprived. These inferior feelings are only confirmed when they are compared to other children whom they perceive to be "better."

Comparing children to friends, brothers, or sisters produces conflict and discouragement. It causes them to want to tattle on others in order to justify themselves and boost their own sense of worth, to make themselves look good, or to get even with the other children. Tattling needs to be ignored. Overexplaining, arguing, or overreacting to tattlers gives them the reinforced attention they want and promotes further tattling. But removing the need for tattling by avoiding comparison with others is an even more satisfactory solution.

Objective #6: Recognizing Unrealistic Expectations and Ambitions Which Discourage.

Parents quite naturally want their children to excel in school, sports, activities, and personal accomplishments. But an overambitious drive to see them successful makes unrealistic demands upon growing children and adolescents. Children seldom question our expectations; rather, they question their own adequacies. They measure success by their ability to please us. Overly high standards can undermine their sense of self-worth.

Children need to know what is expected of them. We need to set limits, teach values, and establish rules, but *only* when they are based upon realistic expectations. Unnecessary regulations and demands produce rigidity in children, a feeling that they are never quite good enough. This self-defeating attitude in turn creates a fear of new experiences. Children who feel they can never quite measure up are reluctant to make new friends or attempt new activities, because they fear rejection and humiliation.

There is nothing wrong with wanting the best for our children. But it is a good idea for us to examine our expectations, to make sure we are not being unrealistic or overdemanding. We also need to remember that children need frequent assurance from us that they are OK, even when they fail to meet our expectations. It is important that they know their attempts to improve are just as important as their final accomplishments.

Objective #7: Making Affirmation Statements.

Learning to convey love and acceptance to our children by making affirmative statements about them is one of the most important skills a parent can learn. As Dr. Haim Ginott suggests in his book, *Between Parent and Child,*

> Such descriptive statements and the child's conclusions are the building blocks of mental health. What he concludes about himself in response to our words, the child later restates silently to himself. Realistic positive statements repeated inwardly by the child determine to a large extent his good opinion of himself and the world around him.[5]

Dr. James Mallory suggests that much unnecessary family tension could be avoided if parents would learn to verbally acknowledge their children's contributions and efforts:

> It is particularly important that parents give positive affirmation to their children. Many young people have told me that the

only time they get any attention is when they are doing something wrong. We need to give them recognition and praise when they do well. Furthermore, when they act from good motives, we should praise them even if the performance is not always that outstanding. How many children have been disillusioned and discouraged because even when they try to do something good, they are criticized for it![6]

Children feel useful and special when we express our appreciation of them. But not all *praise statements* build up confidence or make children feel secure and worthwhile. Actually, some statements may give cause for discouragement or misbehavior. If children feel embarrassed by or unworthy of a compliment, they will react in such a way as to deny the praise.

For this reason, Dr. Ginott suggests that recognition be directed toward effort and improvement rather than personality attributes. For example, children can be told how much we think of their work rather than how "good" we think they are. If our child cleans the yard, we could say, "The yard looks terrific; I really appreciate you and all the hard work you've put in today," instead of, "Hey, you really are a good kid to do that for me."

Statements like the first one affirm; those like the second merely flatter. Flattery doesn't motivate the way sincere positive appreciation does; it appeals to pride and implies conditional acceptance ("If you *don't* do that for me, you're *not* a good kid!"). Affirmation recognizes the effort and behavior of children without drawing any conclusions about their characters.

The following examples show clearly the difference between flattery and affirmation:

DISCOURAGING (FLATTERY) STATEMENTS	ENCOURAGING (AFFIRMATION) STATEMENTS
"You're such a good worker; you really do that well."	"I like the way you handled that; mind if I watch?"

"You're mother's little helper." (The child may not feel he or she deserves that much praise.)

"I appreciate your help; it means a lot to me." (This gives an opinion; there are no expectations to live up to. The child does not have to feel obligated to do well every time in order to be accepted. He or she is motivated to do well—his or her best.)

"You always do well, so don't worry yourself."

"Knowing you, I'm sure you'll figure it out and do just fine."

"You're great at making decisions."

"I have confidence in your judgment. I like the way you go about making your choices."

"You're almost doing that perfectly; it won't be long until you're really a pro."

"You're making good progress and that really counts! It seems to me that you really work hard and are moving right along. It feels good to learn new ways of doing things, doesn't it?"

"You're very good at helping others. Keep up the great work and you'll make me happy."

"Thanks a lot; that was very thoughtful of you to help. I'd like to see you use your talents to help others like you did for me."

The affirmation statements listed above show children that they are valued and accepted by focusing on their accomplishments and not on their personalities. Phrases like these express confidence in the child; they acknowledge any practical or positive effort with sincere appreciation. Here are some other helpful statements which focus on encouragement and affirmation:

"I'm glad you seem to enjoy your work."

"What do you think you can do so that you'll be happier with it?"

"I appreciate you and what you are doing." (Unconditional acceptance.)

"You make my work faster and easier; thanks for helping."

"Since you enjoy making picnic lunches, would you like to help plan and fix a family outing this weekend?"

"That's an interesting idea." (". . . to me"—opinion implied.)

"How did you get that done so quickly?"

"Can you tell me more? Sounds like fun."

"That's right; you're catching on . . . keep going."

"That shows a lot of effort on your part."

In trying to make affirmation statements, parents would do well to keep these two principles in mind: (1) Look for ways to eliminate negative "put down" messages and to focus on statements and attitudes which build good feelings. There are no final answers or perfect rules, but the guidelines we've reviewed can be helpful in learning to communicate with our children more positively. (2) Be realistic about what can be learned in one day, and try not to change too many old habits in a short time.

Verbal affirmation statements don't always come naturally. But we can learn by understanding *how* to make positive statements, and we can profit from our own failures and mistakes. The examples given by others can help us too. In the next two chapters we will look in more depth at the process of communicating with our children.

A FOUNDATION OF ENCOURAGEMENT

Every day we as parents are confronted with opportunities for encouraging or discouraging our children. How we respond to those opportunities can have a profound effect on how our children view themselves all their lives. In her book, *Power for Living,* Joyce Landorf shares this moving illustration:

> One of the most precious things my mother developed in me was the sense of wonder.
>
> I guess all children are born with a sense of wonder, but to reach adulthood with it intact and fully matured is practically a miracle.
>
> I was only a second- or third-grader when I first noticed a field of yellow dandelions while on my way home from school one day. I waded into that glorious golden sea of sunshine, picked all the blossoms my hands could hold, and ran all the way home. I flung the door open wide and shouted, "Here, Mother, these are for you!"
>
> At that moment, my mother was engaged in a Bible study with a roomful of ladies from our church. She had two options: shush me up, or develop my sense of wonder.
>
> In slow magnificent awe she laid her books on the table, knelt beside me, and took my gift.
>
> "Oh, they are beautiful, beautiful, beautiful," she said over and over again. (She could have told me they were messy weeds.) "I love them because you gave them to me." (She could have given me a lecture on picking flowers on private property.) "I'm going to set them on our table for our centerpiece tonight." (She could have told me they'd never last the afternoon and aside from drooping would make my father sneeze.)[7]

Being an encouraging parent doesn't always come naturally. But an encouraging parenting style *can* be learned. Good intentions can gradually mature into new ways of behaving towards our children and communicating with them. When we accept ourselves and our children, when we avoid double standards and guilt peddling, when we learn to separate the deed from the doer, refuse to compare our children, reject unrealistic expectations, and practice verbal affirmation, we give our children a foundation of encouragement that will last them their entire lives.

6 | *I Can't Talk to You Any More*

**LEARNING TO
COMMUNICATE
TOGETHER**

It's midafternoon. You've decided to come home early. You want to surprise the family by taking them out to dinner and to a movie. You've thought about it all week and you've arranged your work schedule to have some time off. You'll finally have a chance to do some family fun things together!

As you slip in the back door, the sound of voices stops you. Out on the patio you hear your fifteen-year-old daughter talking with her friend.

"I can't talk to Mom and Dad any more; they just don't listen. They can't even talk to each other."

Her friend replies, "You really ought to try again, maybe they'll understand how you feel."

"No, all Dad can think about is what he's interested in. For some reason he thinks we should be happy because of what he achieves. He says that he does it for us, but I think

69

that's a cop-out so that he feels better about how he spends his time."

You listen on as your mind races back . . . you begin to reevaluate your motives, your goals, your convincing arguments for justifying your push toward success. You remember the promises you made to yourself and begin to see that you've lost a lot of time building your family life and reaching family goals.

Your daughter continues, "I can't seem to get my ideas across to my parents. Even when they *seem* to listen, it all comes out confused. I end up being frustrated and they end up winning. When I ask them for help, they just lay their opinions on me and tell me how I *should* think and feel. I don't feel that it's safe to share my true feelings. It's like our whole family is wearing masks and playing games. Even Mom and Dad have started arguing most of the time they're together."

Then you remember—just a few days before, your wife said to you, "I'm lonely, I need to talk with you. . . . Couldn't we go out, just the two of us? We don't seem to take time for us any more." (That's when you decided you were going to make a change and spend more time with your wife and children.)

You are shocked, hearing things of which you were not aware. It's frightening, but for a change, you want to be honest. You're admitting to yourself that time is not the only problem. For years you haven't been fully *listening* or *relating—hearing with understanding.* Suddenly it begins to matter deeply. But *how* do you listen? How do you communicate more effectively with your spouse and with your family?

COMMUNICATION BEGINS AT HOME

Obviously, not only dads need help—we all need to learn how to communicate effectively. Communication is essential for building relationships—with ourselves, with our marriage partners, with our children, and with God. But good communication doesn't always come naturally. Life is full of changes, problems, responsibilities, and demands. Stress, pressure, and the misuse of time all can hinder our efforts to communicate and relate, especially as parents.

Various professions in our society have long recognized the importance of relating effectively to both children and adults. Special training is usually required for those who work with children outside the home—teachers, counselors, doctors, social and church workers. In the business world, thousands of dollars are spent helping employees communicate more effectively. But training, experience, and understanding in how to communicate as a family are often taken for granted.

In this chapter we will be looking at various kinds of communication, and examining the quality of communication in different family relationships. It has been my experience that parents who take time out to learn communication skills soon see the benefit of improved communication in their family lives. Many of those who've gone through a series of counseling sessions or who've participated in personal growth groups and learned some communication skills have related, "How we wish we could have had an experience like this before our children reached the age they are now. But we just didn't seem to have the time or think it was important."

Many do not take time to examine their lives until there is a crisis. But how much better to work on improving communication in the back-and-forth of everyday life. Now is the time to evaluate and improve our communication skills!

WHAT IS COMMUNICATION?

Communication involves all our behavior, our words, and the meanings behind what we say and do. Even silence is communication. Everything we do or do not do, say or do not say, sends a message. It is impossible not to communicate.

Of course, words are the most obvious means of communicating with others. Scripture speaks of the power words have to harm or heal:

> Job complained in frustration, "How long will you torment me, and crush me with your words?" (Job 19:2).

> The tongue is small in size but can cause enormous damage. . . . It can use words to control the direction of your relationships and your destiny. Both words of blessing and cursing can come from the same mouth (James 3:7–10).

> A person has joy by the answer he speaks. . . . It's wonderful and rewarding to say the right words at the right time (Proverbs 15:23).

Even though verbal expression can reveal a great deal, it is just one aspect of communication. From his research on communication, Albert Mehrabian concluded that there is a definite meaning and message communicated beyond the use of words themselves. Our *style* of communication can have a greater impact than the words alone. Mehrabian states that only 7 percent of speech is made up of words alone; 38 percent consists of tone of voice and inflection, and 55 percent of facial expressions, posture, gestures, behaviors, and inferences![1]

No wonder that it is sometimes difficult to know exactly what is being communicated. One of the greatest difficulties in communication between individuals is recognizing what the other person really means. There are many instances in which the message received is not the message sent. Our communication often recalls those lines quoted on posters, greeting cards, and cartoons:

> I know you believe that you understand
> what you think I said,
> but I'm not sure
> you realize that
> what you heard
> is not what I meant!

Communication foul-ups occur in families as well as other relationships. And such breakdowns in communication disrupt life for everyone; they affect our personal, spiritual, and marital growth. Learning to overcome the barriers between ourselves and others by developing the qualities and skills of good communication is essential for building a healthy marriage and family life.

LEVELS OF COMMUNICATION

Communication occurs at several different levels, often simultaneously. The first step in understanding how to improve our communication with others is to look at the five levels on which we communicate with our spouses, close friends, and family.

Several years ago I read John Powell's book, *Why Am I Afraid To Tell You Who I Am?*[2] Almost without exception, I ask my clients to read this book during the process of counseling. The most important section for aiding skills in communication is his discussion of the five levels of relating to others.

These five levels, ranging from shallow cliches to deep personal sharing, represent five degrees of willingness and ability to disclose ourselves to others. Briefly listed, in reverse order from the most shallow to the most profound, they are:

5. Fear or friendly cliche level,
4. Factual level,
3. Firm level,
2. Feeling level,
1. Freeing level

Level #5: Fear or Friendly Cliche Level.
This is the level of cliche conversation. When we communicate on this level, we keep ourselves safe by speaking only superficially. We talk in such ways as to protect ourselves and to assure our security and distance. Silence or meaning-

less phrases are used to keep others from knowing how we feel.

At the early stages of relationship, this kind of communication has purpose—it establishes contact. But fear, apathy, feelings of superiority, or poor self-image can keep us at this level. We may at times even want to become close, but fall into phrases which let us hide behind superficial words.

Level five communication in the parent-child relationship reflects indifference, lack of concern, or withdrawal:

With spouses the phrases might sound like:

It is easy to let such phrases become trite acknowledgments with little intention of answering or really sharing one's feelings or experiences.

I'm not suggesting that superficial talk doesn't have its place in families. Level five phrases like these sometimes are necessary; they say, in effect, "I'm busy but I know you're there." The danger lies in making superficial conversation the steady diet of family conversation.

Level five communication outside our families consists of "elevator talk" like this:

Sometimes this kind of talk implies a feeling of superiority, or says, "I'm too busy to stop and converse seriously." At other times, such expressions are necessary or helpful for conveying genuine friendliness at work, church, or in passing, but they do not cultivate closeness. Continuing to use level five communication creates distance between people.

Level #4: Factual Level.

Protective conversation continues behind the screen of reporting the facts about what others are saying or doing. Gossip, narrations, quotes, and events are reported, but nothing personal, and nothing from a feeling level:

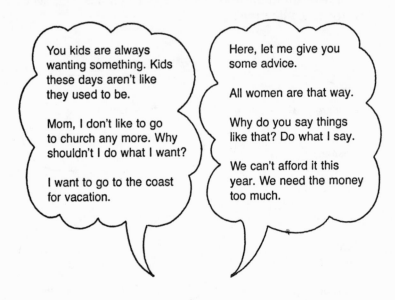

> You kids are always wanting something. Kids these days aren't like they used to be.
>
> Mom, I don't like to go to church any more. Why shouldn't I do what I want?
>
> I want to go to the coast for vacation.

> Here, let me give you some advice.
>
> All women are that way.
>
> Why do you say things like that? Do what I say.
>
> We can't afford it this year. We need the money too much.

This kind of conversation is usually cold and indifferent. There is no sharing of personal feelings or concern for others, no commitment or meaningful content. Level four communication sounds like the six o'clock news. There are more details than in level five conversations, but the talk rambles and goes nowhere.

Level #3: Firm Level.

This is the level at which we begin to express ideas, judgments, opinions, and decisions. When we communicate at level three, we begin to reveal some personal feelings, but still there is caution. At this level we still want to be sure that we're safe, that we'll be accepted along with our ideas and opinions. If we sense rejection, we retreat or say what we think others want to hear.

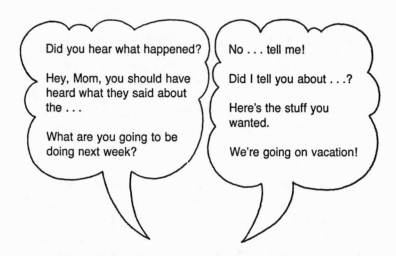

At this level of communication, some risks are taken, but with great concern about image. At times we pretend to be self-confident, assertive, or successful; we would prefer to keep the conversation on an informative basis, rather than disclose our real personality and feelings.

Level #2: Feeling Level.

At this level *feelings* about the facts and opinions which are being expressed are shared more openly. *Sharing* allows openness in conversations; genuine friendships can be cultivated. Fear subsides, threat decreases, trust grows, and rapport is established. We become more assertive, but also more *caring* in our confrontations. We also discover our own uniqueness as we disclose our feelings, needs, desires, motives, and goals.

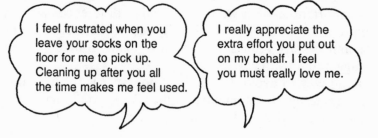

When we communicate on a feeling level, *empathy* begins to build, and there is understanding, affirmation, warmth, and acceptance. Others feel free to respond to us. Authentic relationships become our goal and our experience. Even though others may speak to us from other levels, we respond concretely from within ourselves.

John Powell calls this kind of communication "gut-level" honesty and sharing. It means that we remove masks and share our caring concerns and opinions in ways that build meaningful relationships. Powell summarizes this level of communication by stating:

> Most of us feel that others will not tolerate such emotional honesty in communication. We would rather defend our dishonesty on grounds that it hurts others, and having rationalized our phoniness into nobility, we settle for superficial relationships.[3]

In speaking of emotional honesty, we need to remind ourselves that critical, blunt, or abrasive judgment is not "open honesty." *How* we disclose our "honest" feelings is as important as what we say. There is a difference between appropriate disclosure and indulgence in destructive anger or unnecessary criticism. "Brutal or blunt truth" is often exaggerated truth.

One way to avoid destructive "honesty" is to share our feelings using "I-statements," rather than "you-judgments" that sound critical and may not be true:

You-Judgments	I-Statements
"You make me angry."	"I feel angry."
"You're judging me and reject-ing me."	"I feel rejected by the looks you're giving me."
"You're trying to run my life."	"I want the freedom to choose for myself."

Chapter 8 will explain the specific application of these kinds of statements to the parent-child relationship.

When we communicate on a feeling level, we take responsibility for our feelings and choices. We say, in effect:

I am responsible for choosing my responses to you.
I am responsible for my behavior and feelings.
I am responsible for how I perceive you.
You cannot make me angry unless I choose to be angry.
You cannot make me discouraged, disgusted, or depressed. These are choices I make in reaction to you.
You cannot make me hate; I must choose to hate. You cannot make me jealous; I must choose envy.

And we are free to choose loving responses. We are free to act in concerned, understanding ways, which we choose when we value others and their rights.

Level #1: Freeing Level.

At this level we find personal freedom in sharing, caring, and responding. Deep, authentic friendships and intimate relationships are based on continual, consistent, open, and honest communiction—level one communication. It is the nearest we can get to complete emotional and personal communion. As humans, we can never be at this level permanently. But there are moments and occasions in which we attain almost "perfect" feelings of mutual empathy. We feel free, creative, trusted, understood, cared for, shared with, joyful, tearful, happy, and responsive. Our spirits touch. We are loved for who we are. Language alone cannot picture this depth of experience . . . we can only approximate it:

Perhaps one of the best descriptions I've read of communication on levels one and two is found in a poem entitled "Commitment." It could also be called "Caring" or "Listening," or given many other meaningful names.

I Promise

I will listen to you
I will care about you
I will meet you—

somewhere in the space between us.
If you will step out, I'll find you.
I will not violate your privacy;
 I will wait for you.
I will not make up my mind about what
 you are saying until *you* have said it.

I Promise

I will quiet everything in me that moves—
 my thoughts,
 my feelings,
 my reactions,
I will bring all that is within me to such
 a point of stillness that the only
 thing happening is me.
I will share with you what I learn of
 myself.
I will bring all that is within me to such
 a point of quietness that the only
 thing happening is you.[4]

EVALUATING LEVELS OF COMMUNICATION

A relationship is only as meaningful and effective as its level of communication. Our goal of becoming responsible and encouraging Christian parents cannot be reached unless we attempt to develop communication on levels one and two—which are similar in terms of the use of feelings and openness—in our relationships with ourselves, with our spouses, our children, and our God. An honest assessment of our present levels of communication in these four areas of relationship is an important first step toward improving family communication. It might be helpful to ask ourselves certain questions as we honestly evaluate our communication levels:

Question #1: How do I communicate within myself?
How do I talk to myself and about myself? Who am I?

What are my ideas, needs, wants, goals, values, secrets, frustrations, hurts, cares, and concerns?

As the poem, "Commitment," indicates, only to the degree that we explore ourselves can we bring ourselves to levels two and one in our communication with others. An inner dialogue is often necessary to increase our capacity for communication with others. We will explore this idea further in chapter 7.

Question #2: How do I communicate with my partner?

How does he or she relate to me? Do we listen to each other? Do we hear one another? How do we relate? Do I want to listen? Hear? Relate? Grow intimately? Care? Understand?

Dishonesty causes barriers and defensive reactions between marriage partners. Sharing is often difficult, but in order for a marriage to grow, it is important that there be understanding and acceptance of one another as persons. Otherwise, marriage reverts to a childish stage characterized by bickering, jealousy, and hurt feelings.

Question #3: How do I communicate with children?

What is my understanding of communication not only with my own children, but with other children? Do I remember what it was like to be a child? How did my parents communicate with me? Do I listen to my children? Care? Respond? Do I tune in to hear with an inner ear? Do I see and understand their feelings, ideas, hurts, anger, and struggles?

How we communicate with our children affects how they feel about themselves and how they learn to communicate with others. When we listen and respond, we need to focus on the child and his feelings. It's difficult to always be aware of life from a child's point of view. Parents must choose to attend to a child's concerns in a loving, firm, and kind manner. An atmosphere in which a child's expression is considered as valid as parental expressions promotes closeness and understanding.

Question #4: How do I communicate with God?

How do I perceive him? How do I listen to him? How

does he communicate with me? What do I learn about myself, my spouse, and my children by the way I communicate with God?

Norman Wright, in his book, *Communication: Key to Your Marriage,* summarizes his discussion of communication with God on levels one and two by saying:

> What is it that really frees a person to open his life to another, to reach out to share and to love another person? Before we can love someone else, we must have had two basic experiences in our lives. First of all, we must have experienced love from someone else, and then we must also love ourselves. But what if we grew up never having experienced the true unconditional love that is necessary for us to begin loving ourselves?
>
> 'We love, because He first loved us' (1 John 4:9–11, 18, 19). The ability to love yourself and other people is the result of God reaching out and loving you first. When you accept God's forgiveness and acceptance, you experience His love.[5]

Prayer is communication with God—whereby we receive the power, encouragement, and confidence to face the difficult circumstances in life. It is the channel of communication through which comes the enabling power to communicate with others.

COMMUNICATION IS A
LEARNING PROCESS

Learning to evaluate our present communication levels is an important first step in improving family communication. But learning *how* to change our level of communication is a gradual process. Here are several important communication skills to strive for:

1. To learn to listen to what others say and feel;
2. To learn to clarify incoming messages, to see beyond the words to what is actually being expressed;

3. To focus on the person when listening and the problem when responding;
4. To understand and show concern in a way that lets the other person know that his feelings are important, and that our empathy is genuine;
5. To clearly communicate our feelings to others by accurate feedback.

7 | *If You Love Me, Listen*

**LEARNING
THE ART OF
ACTIVE
LISTENING**

As we have seen in the previous chapter, communication is an essential part of family life. Learning to communicate effectively with our children is one of the most valuable investments we can ever make. And learning successful communication skills begins with learning how to listen. Listening and responding with understanding represents the simplest definition of effective communication.

The little book, *Hey God, Listen!,* by Roxie and Jim Gibson, captures the yearning of a young child's heart to be loved, accepted, and listened to:

Hey God! It's really neat to know you're up this early and ready to listen again! The sun's so warm coming through the window and I know that all is well as long as you're watching over us. I haven't always known that you were watching over us until one day I *really* needed someone to *listen to me,* and you know, God, you were the only one who wasn't busy. You never tell me "Later on," or "Come back when I'm not so busy."

Anyway, God, my teacher said that she was really fed up with me using "anyway" and "you know," but I know you don't mind me using it all the time. You know, God, you're the *only* person I know that loves me just like I am! And that's great![1]

We all need to be listened to—openly, attentively, without judgment or condemnation. Listening is one of the most powerful ways to show acceptance. If someone special to us listens to what we are saying, we feel valued and encouraged. When parents make themselves available to listen, children feel accepted. A child who is listened to hears and feels the message:

"You are important."

"You are special."

"You are loved for who you are, just the way you are."

"You can share all your feelings and I will listen and try to understand."

"You can count on me to be there to help you discover who you are and how important you are to me."

"You won't be judged, rejected, or put down because of who you are and how you feel."

"Your ideas and feelings are unique."

"I have confidence in you."

"You can trust me to care about who you are and how you feel."

Parents who learn the art of listening become predictable and trustworthy in the eyes of their children. Parents who don't listen, on the other hand, promote distrust. In homes where parents don't listen, both parents and children become frustrated and self-centered, trying to outmaneuver each other and gain control. But parents who are committed to listen will find that, with the lines of communication open, control is not an issue. The more we show our children, by listening to them, that we value their thoughts and feelings, the more they will value and respect what we say to them.

It's easy to see that listening is an important part of communication within the family. But being effective and skillful listeners is not a simple proposition. As Jesus himself pointed out in Matthew 13:9–18, effective listening means much more than simply hearing:

> The person who has ears to hear, let him hear . . . let him listen . . . for he can understand what others are not able to. Some have hardened their hearts and do not want to understand. They go through life with their eyes open, but see nothing; with their ears open, but understand nothing of what they hear. How fortunate you are to have eyes that perceive, and ears that hear with understanding from the heart. Listen . . . and understand what I speak to you.

Communication specialists point out that, when a person speaks, there are actually eight facets to the message:

1. What the person is *thinking* and *feeling*.
2. What he *means* to say.
3. What he *actually* says.
4. What he does *nonverbally* that influences the meaning of what he's trying to say.
5. What the listener *hears* or *thinks he hears*.
6. What the listener *interprets* from the verbal and nonverbal message.
7. What the listener *adds* to the message because of his own feelings, experiences, or perceptions.
8. What the listener says in *response*.

Effective listeners take all these facets into consideration. In effect, good listening—hearing with understanding—is the predisposition of the mind and will to hear the feelings, message, and meaning behind another's words. We've all been aware of the person who seems preoccupied with what he or she wants to say the moment we finish speaking; really listening frees us from ourselves and from our own interests long enough to see and feel what others are relating. We are then free to share openly with others, because we have established mutual respect, rapport, and understanding.

For parents, effective listening focuses on the child, rather than on any problem at hand. It involves learning to be aware of things from a child's point of view, directing attention to his feelings, ideas, and concerns. Listening is not passive; it is an active process of reaching out and caring—responding, clarifying, and expressing acceptance and understanding.

Listening allows us to know ourselves and each other—it is a way of loving. Listening is surely a way for parents to love their children.

LEARNING TO LISTEN

How we learn to listen to our children will affect how they feel about themselves and how they learn to listen to others. But learning the art of effective listening takes time and effort. In the remainder of this chapter I want to explore five specific listening skills that can help us in our efforts to become better, more creative communicators with our children.

Listening Skill #1: Create an Atmosphere of Acceptance By Making Neutral or Door-Opener Statements.

These statements indicate acceptance and understanding by implying "tell me more about what you think and feel." They serve as a means for clarification; they "check out" whether we actually understand what the child is trying to express. (What a child says is not always his entire message.) Door-opener responses elicit further cooperation from the child. Neutral responses allow for flexibility and time to focus on the child's true feelings and on both his verbal and nonverbal expressions.

Examples of neutral or door-opener statements are:

"Tell me more about it."
"I'm not sure I know the answer. I'll need some time to

think about it. Talk to me more and tell me your opinion."
"I'd like to know more about how you feel about it first."
"Let me think a second."
"That deserves a lot more consideration than a quick 'no,' so tell me more."
"Let's talk about it."
"Sounds like this is really important to you."
"I just don't know. . . . what do you think?"
"What are your feelings about it?"
"What will it accomplish?"
"Hold on until I can give it some thought."
"Your dad and I will have to talk that over. Tell me more about how you feel so we can decide."

Gradually, each of us will learn how to create expressions which fit his or her own particular style. The old "generation gap" feelings will dissipate as we remain open to our children. The more we open our hearts and minds, the more our children will be encouraged to share freely. Neutral or door-opener statements help us do this because they imply, "I might learn something from you if I listen."

Listening Skill #2: Acknowledge Nonverbal Cues.

We listen by hearing more than just verbal expressions. Nonverbal cues often tell far more than words; such cues are eye contact, facial expression, length of sentences, voice intonation, displayed emotion, body posture, body contact, and so on. Picking up on nonverbal communication requires our undivided attention—this is another way of demonstrating to a child how much we value and accept him.

In acknowledging nonverbal cues, we must try to catch the meaning behind a smile, or a tearful face, or a sullen look. We might respond:

"Your frown seems to tell me that you are hurt about what I said."
"Your smile says that you really like spending time with me."

"It looks like you are having a hard time today. Do you want to tell me how you feel?"

"Your words seem to be saying one thing, but the expression on your face tells me I'm missing your point."

Listening Skill #3: Make Use of an Inner Dialogue.

To help children by listening, we must attempt to enter their world, to experience them as they see and experience themselves. We need to see the reasons and feelings behind what they do, to respond to them with *understanding* and *empathy*.

In order to understand and empathize with a child, we need to reflect on what he or she is saying or doing, to carry out a kind of dialogue with ourselves about what is being communicated. Listening parents will ask themselves questions such as:

"What is the child actually saying?"

"What is the real meaning behind the words?"

"What is the child feeling?"

"What am I feeling?"

"How can I respond from within my own feeling levels?"

"How can I keep our conversation open and helpful without being judgmental or rejecting?"

"How can I understand and be more understanding?"

As we consider these questions, we need to remain as open-minded as possible, suspending judgment until we know we have gotten the full message. Premature assumptions hinder the accuracy of our understanding.

The inner dialogue should go on continually during the process of listening. It is what makes effective listening "active," and it is the key to really understanding our children and ourselves.

Listening Skill #4: Respond with Reflective Statements.

When confronted by a child's expression of hurt or embarrassment—or any strong feeling—many parents react with extremes of expression, saying either, "What did you do? I bet you deserved it. I told you that your sassy tongue was going to get you into trouble," or, at the opposite end of the continuum, "Oh, I'm so sorry, poor sweetheart. Come, let me love you."

It is more productive, and more helpful to the child, to share our understanding of the feelings we perceive he may be experiencing:

"It must have been terribly embarrassing."
"You must feel badly hurt."
"You must have hated yourself and wanted to hide somewhere."
"You must feel furious at her."

Children's feelings are their reasons for choosing their behaviors. But children don't always understand their own feelings, or why they behave as they do. We can help them understand themselves—and at the same time provide an atmosphere of empathy and acceptance—by learning to make reflective statements.

Reflective statements are listening responses which serve as mirrors, enabling children to see themselves more clearly.

> The function of a mirror is to reflect an image as it is, without adding flattery or faults. . . . From a mirror we want an image, not a sermon. . . . The function of an emotional mirror is to reflect feelings as they are, without distortion:
>
> "It looks as though you are very angry."
> "It sounds like you hate him very much."
> "It seems that you are disgusted with the whole set-up."
>
> To a child who has such feelings, these statements are most helpful. They show him clearly what his feelings are. Clarity of image, whether in a looking glass or in an emotional mirror, provides opportunity for self-initiated grooming and change.[2]

Reflective statements are natural outgrowths of the listener's inner dialogue. For instance, when a child says, "I hate school," our first impulse might be to react with:

"Don't say that! You know you really like school. It's no good to hate. You'd better learn to appreciate your education or you'll be sorry."

But when we ask ourselves, "What am I feeling when he says that?" and "What is he feeling?", we are able to listen to the *real* message, and respond with a statement that helps the child understand what the real problem is:

"You're feeling really angry. It looks like you're feeling hurt about something. What happened?"

Learning reflective expression takes practice. What we hear, see, and feel as we listen needs to be expressed verbally; we must learn how to communicate to our children our understanding of their feelings. One help in doing this is to develop a feeling-word vocabulary; the more feeling words that are available to us, the better our chances of understanding our children's experiences and clarifying them verbally.

7-1 is a list of feeling words, arranged in categories for ease of memorization.[3]

Table 7-1
Feeling Words

POSITIVE	SAD	SCARED	CONFUSED	ANGRY
loved	unloved	fearful	trapped	annoyed
glad	down	threatened	undecided	uptight
appreciated	hurt	uncertain	incapable	put out
comfortable	guilty	nervous	troubled	furious
pleased	depressed	anxious	mixed up	accused
encouraged	discouraged	lost	blocked	hate
satisfied	defeated	tense	worried	hurt
proud	bad	eager	torn	miserable
grateful	hopeless	surprised	distressed	rejected
friendly	alone	weak	frustrated	harassed
excited	disappointed	jittery	exhausted	bitter
elated	bored	hemmed in	misunderstood	tense
confident	defeated	insecure	disorganized	bothered

These feeling words can be inserted in response sentences such as:

"You feel ———." (Choose your feeling response.)
"You feel angry at yourself."
"You feel confident within yourself."
"You feel unhappy about who you are."

This response should focus on how the child is feeling about himself.

Using reflective statements may seem unnatural, awkward, or frustrating at first. But once we experience the benefits and see the change in our children's behavior, we will become convinced that our time has been wisely invested.

Listening Skill #5: Keep responses open and nonjudgmental.

The purpose of using good listening skills is to encourage our children to open up and share themselves with us. Keeping the lines of communication open is essential in building any healthy relationship. Rejecting a child's feelings, cutting conversations short, or creating discouragement and misunderstandings closes communication. In contrast, allowing feelings to be expressed without lectures or advice leads to openness in conversations. In the process of listening, we need to keep our responses tentative in order to maintain an open and flowing conversation.

Open responses need not be verbal. Many times, openness can be expressed through silence, facial expression, gestures, or posture. What is important is responding openly to our children out of awareness of our own feelings as well as theirs, and communicating understanding and empathy to them. Such responses encourage children to believe that we accept their feelings and ideas.

Here are examples of *closed* responses to a child's statement:

CHILD: "Janie is moving. (crying) I'll be all alone. Why does she have to go?"

MOTHER: "All right, crybaby. When are you going to grow up? You know you don't accomplish anything by feeling sorry for yourself."

CHILD: "But mother, I'll really miss her; she's my very best friend. I just won't be happy without her."

MOTHER: "You'll get over it. Don't go crying on my shoulder. For a twelve-year-old, you're really acting like a baby."

In this situation, the mother could have asked herself, "How can I best help her by showing that I care and understand?" A more open response would have been:

"It's hard to be separated from your friends. I know you must miss her already. You feel pretty empty inside knowing she's leaving, and I understand."

A child's feelings need to be taken seriously, even though the situation doesn't seem very significant to the parent. A child believes that his feelings are more important than anything else in life. He needs an opportunity and a relationship in which he can find acceptance to express his hurts and accomplishments. When we keep our responses open, we provide such an emotional atmosphere.

Open responses may not always come spontaneously. We have to make a genuine effort to respond within our own feeling levels, in sensitivity to what our children are feeling. It's important to keep our responses simple; a child is looking for understanding, not lengthy analysis. We must also learn to use discretion, and not overuse reflective statements and feeling words. A child may be merely seeking attention or pity, and using these skills at times might reinforce negative feelings and behavior.

LISTENING BUILDS UNDERSTANDING

Active listening is an excellent tool for encouraging children. Listening to our children provides an atmosphere of acceptance and caring, and it lets us be honest and helpful to our children without dominating them or stifling their initiative. The process of active listening helps us become aware of our own feelings and of our children's feelings, and lets us help them understand what is going on inside them.

One recent conversation comes to mind to illustrate our need to appropriate this process into our relationships with our children:

> "Hey, you really understand me, don't you? It feels good to talk with you. You're the first person *in my life* who has ever understood how I feel."

Coming from a seven-year-old, this statement had a bit of humor in it, but it was an affirming confirmation that I had been successful in relating to him. Taking the time to really listen pays off!

8 | *But Mom, I Didn't Do It*

TEACHING RESPONSIBILITY THROUGH UNDERSTANDING PROBLEM OWNERSHIP

Listening, which provides a sense of understanding and acceptance, nurtures the loving, caring relationships children need to develop healthy self-images and lifestyles. But in order to grow toward full maturity, children need more than love and understanding. Early in their emotional and psychological development, children need to learn to accept *responsibility.*

Irresponsibility comes easily to both children and adults. It is natural to protect ourselves by reeling out excuses and defenses when an exposed mistake might result in shame and embarrassment. Most of us cling to security, recoiling in a blaming stance as we try to cover our inadequacies and shortcomings. We blame society, parents, circumstances, the government, and even God—anything to escape from taking responsibility.

For years psychiatry and psychology have blamed secondary causes for personal problems, misbehaviors—even crimes. Today we see a healthy change of emphasis in the same circles of the helping professions—a change toward responsibility. Professionals are realizing that blaming others lets a person effectively avoid changes of behavior, while accepting responsibility builds self-esteem and opens the door to progressive change of attitude and behavior.

Dr. William Glasser, in his book, *Reality Therapy,* defines responsibility as learning to fulfill our basic personal needs in such a way that we do not deprive others of the ability to fulfill their own needs:

> A responsible person does that which gives him a feeling of self-worth and a feeling that he is worthwhile to others. He is motivated to strive for and perhaps endure privation to attain self-worth.[1]

To feel worthwhile, we need to maintain a satisfactory standard of behavior within ourselves. We must learn to evaluate ourselves, correct ourselves when we do wrong, and credit ourselves when we do right. We must learn to respect others, for as we do this we learn ultimately to respect ourselves. Morals, standards of right and wrong, and values are all specifically related to personal fulfillment, which can only be achieved with a serious commitment toward responsibility.

Jesus emphasized the importance of personal responsibility when he taught that "out of the inner person of a man—his very heart and mind," comes the source of choices to do evil and create problems (Matt. 5:18–20). James 1:19–26 has some appropriate words about accepting responsibility:

> Let every person be quick to listen, but slow to speak . . . slow to lose his temper in anger. Losing your temper doesn't develop godly character. Hearing and knowing is not enough. Put into practice what you hear, for you only deceive yourself when you fail to respond with action to what you already know and understand.

The person who simply hears and does nothing about it is like a person who sees his reflection in the mirror but forgets what he sees. When you listen and understand the truth, *follow through by assuming the responsibility,* lest your hearing has been a waste of time.

Hearing is for producing change and action. God's laws are principles of liberty. To obey God is liberty, and those who obey become responsible, happy people who haved acted upon their knowledge.

TEACHING RESPONSIBILITY

The very nature of childhood is contrary to being adult, responsible, and controlled. But children can—and need to—learn responsibility. Responsibility can be taught by relatives, teachers, ministers, and friends—any responsible persons who create personal involvements with children and teach them "responsibility through the proper combination of love and discipline."[2] But teaching and exemplifying responsibility is a job that falls primarily to parents.

Responsibility in children begins at home with the parents' attitudes, values, manner of communication, skills, and responses. Children learn what they experience in relationship with their parents, and they learn by example. For this reason, our first task in teaching children responsibility is to accept responsibility ourselves. We raise responsible children by being responsible parents.

Responsible parents relate to their children in appropriate ways. They are neither too permissive nor too strict. By their example, they demonstrate ways of coping with feelings and solving problems. When they realize that certain behaviors or attitudes are harmful to themselves and others, they take constructive action to control or eliminate the offense.

Responsible parents openly acknowledge their feelings—"bad" ones as well as "good"—and they allow their children the same privilege. At the same time, they try to practice and exemplify self-control in communication, making an effort to respond to their children in ways that encourage rather than condemn. Conversationally, they use statements which build self-esteem by indicating a belief in their children's capacity to make wise decisions for themselves, responding with affirming statements such as:

"You decide about that."

"Talk to me about it."

"I can't do your homework for you, but I can listen and try to help you understand until you can get it yourself."

"Whatever you decide is fine with us."

"I know you lost your library book. What are you going to do to earn enough money to replace it?"

"You broke the school rules. Tell me how you feel about the restrictions they've put on you. I believe we should suffer the consequences when we fail, but I want to understand your feelings."

"Yes, I'm angry, but I'll try to control myself if you tell me what you want to do to earn my trust again."

As the above statements indicate, responsible parents help children make their own choices, solve their own problems, and use their own personal creative resources. They learn when to intervene and when to withdraw in order for the child to assume full responsibility. Dr. Haim Ginott describes this process in *Between Parent and Child:*

> Education for responsibility is fostered by allowing children a voice, and whenever indicated, a choice, in matters that affect them. A deliberate distinction is made here between a voice and a choice. There are matters that fall entirely within the child's realm of responsibility. In such matters, he should have his choice. There are matters affecting the child's welfare that are exclusively within our realm of responsibility. In such matters, he may have a voice, but not a choice. We make the choice for him . . . while helping him to accept the inevitable.[3]

Promoting responsibility in children is a slow process. It must be taught by example and careful guidance. And it will not always work! As parents who are at times immature themselves, we have no right to expect our children to behave maturely all the time. To demand that a child always behave perfectly and control her wants, feelings, and frustrations all the time is unrealistic and damages the child's motivation.

But children *do* learn responsibility when they are treated responsibly:

> Children are not born with a built-in sense of responsibility. Neither do they acquire it automatically at a certain prescribed age. Responsibility, like piano playing, is attained slowly and over many years. It requires daily practice (encouragement and experiences) in exercising judgment and in making choices about matters appropriate to one's age and comprehension. . . .[4]

Parents who encourage this process are parents who will promote their children's growth toward full maturity.

WHO OWNS THE PROBLEM?

Teaching responsibility requires serious effort in order to see progress in a child's growth toward independence and maturity. Parents who struggle to be responsible themselves and to break old habit patterns need specific guidance as to *how* to respond to their children in ways that encourage responsibility, especially when difficulties arise. One very helpful way to assess situations and determine what tactics to use in order to encourage responsibility is to learn to ask, "Who owns the problem?"

Problem ownership refers to the question of who is experiencing difficulty with whom in a specific conflict-causing situation. The person whose needs and wants are not being met is the one who needs to "own" the problem—to claim responsibility for seeking solutions. Thomas Gordon has outlined some basic rules and principles that can be helpful to parents in answering the questions of problem ownership. He outlines three situations that can arise when dealing with children. I will suggest a fourth, based on an

Adlerian and scriptural principle of social and moral responsibility:

1. *There Is No Problem:* The child is satisfying his own needs (he is not thwarted) and his behavior is not interfering with the parents or with others.
2. *The Child Owns the Problem:* The child is thwarted in satisfying his own needs. It is not the parent's problem, because the child's behavior in no way interferes with the parent's satisfying his own needs.
3. *The Parent Owns the Problem:* The child is satisfying his own needs or wants (he is not thwarted). *But* his behavior is a problem to the parents because it is interfering in some specific way with the parents' needs. The parents' right to satisfy their own needs is being blocked.
4. *The Parent or Others Own the Problem:* The child is satisfying his own needs, but in violation of acceptable standards of behavior and the values, rights, rules, and privileges of the parents, family, group, or society— especially if the child desires to be a part of the benefits and protection of that group.

Once we have identified problem ownership in a particular situation, we can take appropriate action. Of course, when there is no problem, when both parents and children are satisfying their own needs without interfering with others, the appropriate response is mutual acceptance and respect. Parents need to be realistic at this point and not be overly demanding of their children. When the child is satisfied and is not infringing on the rights of his parents or of society, he can be left alone!

WHEN THE CHILD OWNS THE PROBLEM

Here are some examples of situations in which the child owns a problem:

—Bob is lonely and wants someone to play with him

—Jane feels inadequate and wants someone to help her do her homework

—Ray doesn't know how to ask a girl for a date

—Child has lost his toy and wants parent to find it

—The kids don't know what to do with their free time

—Janice is feeling shy because of her hesitance to make friends

—Billy says he hates his teachers

—Frank argues and fights with his school friends

—Sue complains about no time to do her homework

In cases like these active listening is the best response parents can make; neutral and acknowledgement statements, inner dialogue, and reflective statements all express care, concern, and empathy while encouraging the child to take responsibility for solving his own problem. Below are some examples of active listening responses to situations in which the child owns the problem:

SITUATION	SUGGESTED RESPONSE
Rob comes home crying about his failure in school.	"You're feeling disappointed about your grades. I can understand that . . . Want to tell me about it?"
Sally feels frustrated because she wants to date and boys don't ask her out.	"It looks to me that you're feeling left out and hurt when guys don't ask you for a date. What do you think their problem is in asking you?"
Rick is upset with a friend for not playing with him.	"You seem angry with him. What do you think you can do to change things?"

Many parents find this concept difficult to accept on a consistent basis. We may begin using listening skills but give in to moralizing or offering solutions prematurely. But when we do this, both we and our children lose; we defeat our goal of teaching them to assume responsibility and solve their own problems. Using responses that encourage problem ownership builds self-confidence in our children by encouraging them to be responsible for resolving their own feelings.

Of course, there will be times when a child needs more help in solving his problems than active listening can give him. Chapter ten will explore problem-solving skills parents can use in helping their children make responsible decisions.

WHEN PARENTS OWN THE PROBLEM

Learning to tell the difference between child-owned problems and parent-owned problems takes some practice. Here are some examples of how problems belonging to the child can become parent's problems:

"THAT'S YOUR PROBLEM" (Child owns the problem; parent uses reflective listening and problem solving techniques to help child find own solution)	"I'VE GOT A PROBLEM" (Parent owns problem, chooses response which openly acknowledges the difficulty but which also puts responsibility on child to change his behavior)
Child is restricted at school.	Child's restrictions become problem to parent in driving carpool home.
Child cries about grades on exam.	Child wants all privileges of other kids but refuses to do his schoolwork.
Child feels he has been given too much homework.	Child interrupts parents in front of guests and begs for help with homework.
Child fails to make ball team.	Child signs up for team when the family rule of not joining had already been agreed upon.

| Child is upset about losing. | Child continually complains and irritates family members about losing. |

In situations where the parents own the problem, it is up to them to assume responsibility for it. But owning a problem involving children also means assuming responsibility for teaching them to respect the rights and feelings of others. Behavior that consistently thwarts the needs of others cannot be accepted. It is important that parents who own a problem communicate that fact clearly to their children.

But *how* the problem is communicated is very important. At times our reactions to our children can cause them to be defensive, overly self-protective, frustrated, or humiliated. Or children can become parent-deaf; they learn to tune us out when all they hear from us is "you-judgments":

"You're impossible."
"You're a bad girl."
"You're stupid."
"You're lazy."
"Don't be ugly" ("you" implied).
"That was a dumb thing to do" ("you" implied).

Not all you-judgments verbalize criticism, shame, blame, or ridicule. Some attempt to produce cooperative behavior by flattery or praise of character:

"You're a good boy."
"You're smart."
"You're nice to do that."
"You were a good kid today."

Both kinds of you-judgments can be damaging to our goal of encouraging children to accept responsibility. A constant diet of judgmental statements causes a child to feel and think, "I've done the wrong thing again, now my parents will hate me." Negative behavior may even be reinforced, and communication becomes stifled. A child longs to believe that, no matter what happens, his parents will always love him.

"Parent-owned I messages" serve that purpose, and are the appropriate response when the parent owns the problem. I-messages describe the child's behavior and how we feel about the problem that it causes us. They do not attack with blame or manipulate with flattery, but rather explain to the child that his or her behavior produces consequences and sometimes strong feelings within the parent. I-messages allow a parent to ventilate anger or other feelings appropriately. They attack the problem instead of the child.

I-message responses vary according to the situation or the relationship, but each I-message generally needs to communicate three ideas. These components can be explicit or implied, and need not be in order:

1. The child's behavior is specifically described as causing a problem: "I want you to stop making noise."
2. The parent's feelings are expressed about the difficulties the problem is causing them: "I get annoyed and angry."
3. The consequences of the problem are stressed so that the child will know the parents' feelings are related to his behavior. The consequence is expressed in a nonthreatening manner which allows choice: "You'll have to choose to do something else if you can't respect my request."

In other words, the I-message:

States the behavior:	"I want you to _____" or "When you _____"
States the feeling:	"I feel _____" or "I get _____"

	"You'll have to _____"
States the consequence:	or
	"You have the choice to ____"

At first parents may find I-messages unnatural, and may find it difficult to conceive how anyone could ever learn to be so calm and exacting in stressful situations. But practice makes these kinds of nonjudgmental responses come more easily. Here are some examples of you-judgments contrasted with I-messages:

YOU-JUDGMENTS	I-MESSAGES
"You're a pain in the neck! You stop that racket this instant or I'll whip you."	"I want you to stop making noise. I've told you before how I feel about being waked up. I get annoyed and angry because you continue to ignore my requests. I've given you a warning. You'll have to go outside to play if you can't play quietly in the house."
"You're a liar."	"I don't think I can count on you when you keep doing the opposite of what you say."
"You're hopeless. I know you can do better than that."	"I feel frustrated because you don't seem to be working up to your potential. I guess you get pretty discouraged too."
"You're the slowest brat in the family."	"I'm leaving in five minutes. Remember the last time I left you home when you weren't ready?"
"You're late again. If you cared anything about anybody but yourself you'd get home on time."	"I try to have dinner ready at a time everyone can eat together. Starting tomorrow, if you're late you'll have to get

	some leftovers out of the refrigerator."
"You're a brat!"	"I can't stand all of this arguing. I won't allow backtalk."
"You're so sloppy. Why don't you ever pick up your clothes?"	"I don't like to pick up your clothes every day. I need some time to think and then I want to talk to you about your problem of causing me extra work. You try to decide what you want to do about it while I try to control my anger and frustration."

Responding with nonjudgmental I-messages involves more than just using all the right words and phrases. We can convert an I-message into a you-judgment nonverbally by displaying anger or hostility in our manner or tone of voice. "I'm tired of interruptions" can be used effectively by a mother to express her inner feelings without attacking the child's self-esteem and character. But the same thing can be said in harshness and hostility in front of others to embarrass the child. The I-message then actually becomes a judgmental "You're rude!" The child may counterattack, since the mother also was rude and disrespectful.

You-judgments are taken by children as rejection. I-messages, on the other hand, effectively influence children to modify their behavior in an acceptable and positive manner, and to take responsibility for their actions. In summary, the I-message:

1. Shows respect for the child's person and feelings.
2. Makes it clear to the child that his behavior is interfering with the rights or needs of someone else.
3. Identifies the parent's view as to what specific problem the child has caused the parent.
4. Acknowledges ownership of the parent's feelings and the reasons for those feelings.

5. Allows the parent to share his feelings without attacking the child.
6. Emphasizes sharing the parent's dilemma rather than blaming the child.
7. Focuses on the child's behavior and retains respect for the parent-child mutual relationship.

WHEN THE PARENT OR OTHERS OWN THE PROBLEM

At first glance this fourth problem category may sound identical to the third. But here we are talking about more than needs or feelings. The parent or others own the problem when the child is satisfying his own needs and wants at the expense of the values and accepted standards of the group of which he is part.

Examples of such situations are:

—Paul takes a quarter from his mother's purse;
—Sally pushes Jane into the mud;
—Pat is discovered cheating on an exam;
—Chris and his friends vandalize an abandoned building.

It is easy to see that situations like these may overlap with those in which the parents own the problem. Pat's behavior may cause her parents to feel ashamed and embarrassed, for instance, or Chris's mother may resent having to pay for the damage her son has caused. But the real issue in these situations is values, not feelings. Parents owe it to their children to teach and exemplify responsibility toward family, society, and God.

The appropriate parental response to situations in which the parent or others own the problem is to make it clear that the nonacceptable behavior will not be tolerated. Active listening and I-message responses are not out of place at this point, but often some form of disciplinary action is needed. One of the best ways to accomplish this is to let the child experience the natural or logical consequences of his action.

We will discuss discipline and consequences in depth in chapters 11 and 12.

RESPONSIBILITY AND PROBLEM OWNERSHIP

Learning to be responsible builds a child's sense of self-confidence and self-worth. Teaching responsibility to our children begins with taking responsibility for ourselves and our behavior, and helping our children take care of their own problems. Learning to determine who owns a problem, to use active listening and problem-solving skills, to own our problem and make I-message responses can help us become models of responsibility for our children. The four categories of problem ownership and the appropriate responses are summed up in table 8-1.

Table 8-1
Problem Ownership Responses

ACCEPTANCE		
	Child owns the problem	Use active listening and problem-solving responses
	There is no problem	Acceptance with mutual respect

NON ACCEPTANCE		
	Parent owns the problem	Use neutral and nonacceptance responses phrased as parent-owned "I messages"
	Parent or others own the problem	Use nonacceptance responses or allow children to experience the consequences

Parents are usually far too eager to take over a child's problem. But quick solutions do not help children learn coping skills or gain appreciation for the resources they have for solving their own problems creatively. Learning to ask "who owns the problem" encourages children by helping them develop and use their own personal and emotional resources in situations where it is appropriate. Determining problem ownership is also a useful tool in helping parents not to overreact to, blame, or lecture a child. It allows parents to set a valuable example for their children of owning and handling problems.

9 | *What Do I Do Now?*

HELPING CHILDREN SOLVE THEIR PROBLEMS

"Talking isn't teaching . . . and telling isn't helping a child to learn . . . because, if talking was teaching, my kids would be Ph.D.s," commented Dr. Howard Hendricks at a conference on communication. Telling our kids what to do, how to do it, when to do it, and why they need to do it doesn't necessarily inculcate them with the ability to make important decisions or solve their own problems.

Making decisions and solving problems are natural experiences of life, unavoidable in the process of growing toward emotional and spiritual maturity. As we have seen in the previous chapter, parents encourage responsibility and build self-esteem in children by allowing them to solve their own problems and make their own decisions. But children can't be entirely self-sufficient, and they sometimes need help in thinking through what they should do in certain situations.

What then is the solution? How do we respond to our children so that we provide the necessary guidance they need without doing all the thinking for them? How can we give them a model or process for problem solving which they will be motivated to internalize? How can our responses guide them so that they learn to explore alternatives, make choices, and assume responsibility for their own problems?

We can help our children learn to make decisions and solve problems if we can learn how to become involved with them through meaningful interaction rather than through constant supervision or intervention. Learning how to do this in decision-making situations will be the focus of this chapter.

STEP BY STEP

Problem solving requires a plan, a step-by-step process which takes us from where we are to where we want to go in a logical, sequential order. We move progressively from step to step, and each step clarifies our choices and builds our confidence in our ability to continue. Each step in the process is as important as the solution itself.

Briefly, the steps to successful problem solving are:

1. Arrive at a summary statement through active listening,
2. Develop insight by exploration and discovery (brainstorming),
3. Prioritize alternatives, decide and choose,
4. Act and evaluate.

Remember, the purpose of this problem-solving sequence is to help children think through their own feelings and problems in order to choose solutions which make sense to them. Open responses and active listening often help children discover solutions quickly; they may find an answer during the first step of the process. However, there are times when children need additional assistance and more specific help in thinking through the alternatives.

This is not to be confused with giving *advice*. Advice says, "Do this!" or "You should do it this way" or "I told you you should have . . ." Advice does not help children learn to solve their own problems; it makes them dependent on their parents. Furthermore, children often resist advice.

Healthy guidance in problem solving encourages children to believe that they have the God-given resources within themselves to evaluate their problems and options. Parents remain actively involved, but avoid "dumping" preconceived ideas or solutions on the child. This does not mean that parents *never* share their values or ideas; there are appropriate times to communicate directly in a nonjudgmental manner. But the primary emphasis must be on helping the children come to their own conclusions.

Step #1: The Summary Statement.

In the previous chapters we discussed how the process of active listening can be applied when children need to own their own problems. At the completion of this process of listening and understanding, we should be able to state the problem briefly and succinctly. This summary statement will be used as a starting point for helping the child solve the problem. Briefly, the summary statement should:

1. Identify or personalize the child's feelings.
2. Specify and personalize the precise situation that has caused the problem.
3. Identify and personalize the child's key concern, lack, need, deficit, failure, or attempted solution, along with any self-defeating ideas he may have.
4. Identify and personalize the child's goal, want, wish, idea, or desired behavior change.

For example:

1. "You feel _____ FEELING
2. about _____or towards _____ SITUATION

3. because you cannot _____or   **PROBLEM**
   lack the ability to _____,
4. and you want to be able to ___.   **GOAL**

Depending on the problem, it could take three to thirty minutes to listen, understand, and arrive at an accurate summary statement. However, until we know the feelings, the situation, the defeating ideas, and the goal, we cannot begin the actual problem-solving process. Through the other problem-solving steps, we continue to use active listening to clarify and identify alternatives.

Step #2: Exploration and Discovery.

At this point we help children develop insight by discussing what they need to do. Our responses need to be specific and communicate confidence in the children's ability to come up with their own ideas. It is important not to rush them, but rather to adapt to their pace. At times, because of a lack of experience, children cannot generate plausible ideas; if this happens, we can make tentative suggestions, although these should be kept to a minimum. Occasionally we may have to back up and limit ourselves to reflecting the children's feelings about their ideas. Possible responses at this stage are:

"What are some of the things you'd like to do about this problem?"

"What options do you have?"

"How would you solve that problem?"

"What have you thought about doing?"

"What do you feel about what you could do to change things?"

"What have you tried that didn't work?"

"Let's talk a minute and see if there is any way to work it out."

"Now, let's figure out how you will do this. What are your ideas?"

"What would you like to see take place?"

"What would you like to see changed?"

"How else could you handle that problem?"

"I don't know the answer, but I'll be glad to talk about it. Tell me what your feelings and thoughts are."

"Any other options?"

"What could you say to your friends that might change their minds?"

"I feel confused too, but let's just keep talking a moment and maybe we'll come up with an idea."

"Keep on, I think you've got some good ideas."

"Have you considered . . ."

"Let's make a list of things you could do."

"How do you think I'd handle that kind of situation? Do you like my idea or do you have a better one? I can learn a lot from your ideas too!"

Obviously, these ideas have to be personalized into each situational context. The purpose is to find transitional phrases which encourage a child to explore his own ideas, feelings, and resources. The next step is to begin to prioritize the alternatives, make decisions, and choose a plan to follow.

Step #3: Prioritize Alternatives, Decide and Choose

At this stage we encourage and assist the child to select appropriate alternatives and solutions which will be consistent with his needs, ideas, values, and goals. The child should be made aware of the benefits of choosing the options which produce the most effective long-range solutions rather than immediate gratification or temporary relief. This can be accomplished by discussing the probable results of his choice before he actually attempts his solution. The following are examples of statements which assist a child to evaluate and choose from his various possibilities:

"Which idea do you like the best? Why?"

"Let's summarize and list the ideas you think are best."

"Let's list your thoughts in two columns—first choices, second choices."

"What do you want to do first?"

"Which idea makes the most sense?"

"Which idea do you think you'll try first? For what reason?"

"Which alternative is most likely to fail?"

"What have you decided to do thus far?"

"You seem to be coming up with some good choices. Which one are you going to try first?"

"Why do you think that will work?"

"What do you think will happen if you choose that plan?"

"What if you change your mind later?"

"How will that choice affect you later on? What do you think your friends will say about your choice?"

Step #4: Act and Evaluate.

Once children have made their decisions, we encourage them to act on what they have decided. If it has been their own conclusion and choice, the probability is that their motivation is already built into their decision. Parents should continue to use reflective statements to summarize for the children how they're feeling about the entire decision-making process.

When possible, it is often wise to help a child evaluate the results of his actions. But it is important to allow the child to draw his own conclusions, and not to criticize his failures. Much learning results from making mistakes. Evaluation time is not an occasion for parents to prove that their way would have been better, but for letting the children share their feelings and conclusions.

Remember, our goal is to help children gain emotional and psychological independence and build their confidence in their abilities to be creative and resourceful. Solving problems for our children only frustrates them and discourages them from learning to become responsible for their own emotional, psychological, and spiritual maturity. At times we might feel compelled to remove all consequences and failures from the paths of our children. In the long run, such a habit would prove detrimental. Growth comes from assuming responsibility for our difficulties and receiving appropriate help and encouragement from others. James Dobson relates:

> I would remind you . . . that the human personality grows through mild adversity, provided it is not crushed in the process. Contrary to what you might believe, the ideal environment for your child is not one devoid of problems and trials. I would not, even if I could sweep aside every hurdle from the paths of my children, leaving them to guide along in mirth. They deserve the right to face problems and profit from the confrontation.[1]

It is helpful to remember, as we try to guide our children towards learning to solve their own problems, that God has designed us to grow by facing challenges. Even as we, through prayer, trust in God for help, we learn that he allows us to grow spiritually by working through our problems. If prayer and faith were simply methods of getting things done for us, then they would be detrimental to our character development. But faith is never the easy way out. In fact, it may mean facing the more difficult solutions because we choose to do what is right or best rather than skirting the issue.

Faith is trusting God for the ability to overcome or achieve what seems impossible. Through prayer, God's Holy Spirit responds to us as an "Encourager" or "Helper" who enables us and our children to identify our problems, search out alternatives, and grow in the process of learning to resolve our difficulties.

10 | *Life Looks Different from Three Feet High*

**UNDERSTANDING
GOALS OF
BEHAVIOR**

My friend, Dan Jackson, tells of a humorous incident he witnessed as he walked down the hallway of a church educational building. He saw the teacher of a class of three-year-olds "hanging out the doorway and bursting with laughter."

"What happened?" Dan inquired.

The teacher responded, "One of our little guys just hit his friend and knocked him down!"

"And that's funny?" asked my friend.

"Well," the teacher continued, "when I asked him why he hit his friend, the little boy said, 'Because he wasn't being ye kind unto me.'"

Funny, but illustrative of how children think and feel about situations. Life looks different from a child's perspective. And children have their own "private logic" (or "private illogic," as the case may be) for doing what they do. They are motivated to respond to life situations according to their feelings and personal perceptions. They have needs they want met and self-interests they want to protect. And they behave in ways that to them seem appropriate for getting those needs met and those interests protected.

This is important to realize as we try to understand why our children behave as they do, and as we try to determine the best ways to handle misbehavior. To help children we have to have some understanding of their natures and their thinking processes. We need to understand their feelings about life. Children are whole persons with complex needs, wants, fears, desires, feelings, and questions. As responsible parents we want to encourage them to change their misbehaviors and become responsible, caring persons. As we more clearly understand why they misbehave and learn to recognize the mistaken ideas behind their misbehaviors, we will become better equipped to help them change their negative actions into positive, productive ones.

THE PURPOSE OF BEHAVIOR

Alfred Adler, one of the first psychiatrists to break with Sigmund Freud, taught that every human behavior has a *goal,* and that this goal becomes the explanation for that behavior. Children don't act out of a vacuum; they respond to certain situations in a manner that is based on their personal interpretations and is calculated to achieve certain results. Misbehavior grows out of children's mistaken ideas, beliefs, and assumptions about how they can get what they want, feel worthwhile and important, or gain a sense of love, achievement, belonging, or pleasure. Accordingly, children do not tend to change their behavior unless they understand that it is contributing to their problem and unhappiness. They will not stop annoying behavior until they recognize that it is not being rewarded.

Rudolf Dreikurs, in his classic work, *Children: The Challenge,*[1] expanded on Adler's ideas by classifying children's mistaken goals into four categories:

1. *Attention*—"I don't feel loved, but at least I can feel noticed if I can get others to pay attention to me or serve me."
2. *Power*—"I may not be able to achieve, but I can show others that they can't defeat me or stop me from doing what I want. And they can't make me do what they want."
3. *Revenge*—"Others do not like me, and I'm afraid everyone will reject me, so I'll hurt them first, or strike back when they try to hurt me. I can't be loved, so I'll get even."
4. *Inadequacy*—"Since I can't do what others expect of me, I'll do nothing, so they'll leave me alone. I'll convince them that I'm unable or helpless. I don't like myself and I feel hopeless, so I'll convince others that I can't do anything."

Considering the goals of behavior explained by Adler and his followers can be a useful tool for parents who are struggling to deal with negative behavior in children. At first, the four goals may seem difficult to differentiate, but with practice parents can gain meaningful insights into themselves and their children by learning to ask themselves, "What purpose does my child's misbehavior serve?" Is there a striving for attention, recognition, or acceptance? Is there a struggle for power and control, or an attempt to defeat others? Is there the need to get even and retaliate, or a plea for fairness and justice? Or is there the appearance of fear, helplessness, embarrassment, or rejection? Asking these questions in any particular situation will help pinpoint the goal of the behavior.

It is important to remember that, although behavior is goal-directed and not accidental, children may not always be aware of the motives behind their behavior. Asking them "why" they have behaved a certain way may actually confuse them and make them feel defensive. They may not know the answer, or they may not want to reveal their discouragement and sense of hurt. Asking children "what" they did, "what" they are trying to do, or "what" they feel will be more productive. Active listening will further help uncover their feelings and discouraging assumptions. It will be easier then to discover the purpose their negative behavior is accomplishing for them.

With this in mind, let's consider in more detail the four goals listed by Dreikurs.

ATTENTION

The goal of attention is rooted in a genuine need to be loved. Children usually seek attention in positive ways, but may get discouraged when they feel ignored, put down, useless, or insignificant. They then seek affirmation and the feeling that they're making a useful contribution within the family. Finally, when they feel that they can't achieve a sense of worth by positive behavior, they conclude that they will feel better if they can get others to notice or serve them in a negative way. Attention-seekers may interrupt, disturb, tease, annoy, or frustrate others until those others "pay attention." They have lost confidence in their ability to use socially constructive means to feel significant, and they would rather be reprimanded than be ignored. Humiliation, punishment, and even physical pain don't deter them as long as their goal of attention is achieved.

Children who seek attention may use emotions to get special treatment. When parents console and pamper children out of sympathy, those children come to expect special treatment. They may try to get others to relate to them in similar ways.

For example, Janice whines about going to bed. When her parents express their concern and try to make her feel happy, Janice simply continues to find one excuse after another to delay going to bed. She's not happy unless she can keep her parents busy serving her needs. She assumes no responsibility for feeling satisfied. Her parents' genuine desire to be loving is manipulated by their daughter. They cater to her mistaken idea that being loved means being constantly attended to. Therefore Janice also demands of her playmates that everything be done her way. If she isn't the center of attention, she refuses to play.

Meeting children's obsessive demands may give parents peace, but only temporarily. Those children will probably resume the same behavior later or disturb in another way, because they have been conditioned to make themselves feel worthwhile by getting others to tend to their needs.

If parents feel annoyed, frustrated, distracted, or interrupted by their children's behavior, then the goal is probably attention. Reacting by punishing, reminding, or coaxing simply reinforces the attention-getting goal, because it serves as a reward.

Ignoring children's demands, although it may cause them to give up and search for new ways to entertain and satisfy themselves, does not solve the problem completely. And it does nothing about meeting their genuine needs for love and affirmation.

We can alter our responses in ways which ignore attention-getting devices while motivating children to feel significant because of what they do. We need to praise and reinforce useful contributions and cooperativeness in order to assure the child of his place in the family. We can focus attention on positive behaviors and reject any demands for service. We can be firm, but loving and kind. Understanding the goal of attention can help us discern what options we have, what not to do, and what we can do to encourage rather than discourage our children who feel the need to be noticed.

POWER

"Bill, please pick up your things so we can get ready for the meeting in here tonight," Dad requests. "No! I don't want to— I just got started," Bill argues back. "You will do what I say when I tell you to," Dad replies. "But, Dad, you never let me finish anything. You're always telling me to do something else." Bill responds. Dad threatens, and Bill quickly but reluctantly begins picking up his belongings. He grumbles, "Other kids don't get bossed around like I do." Dad replies, "I don't care what other parents do—you obey me." "You're always picking on me about something," Bill whines. Dad snaps back, "That's enough, young man!"

The goal of power is related to children's genuine need to feel confident, to achieve, to be successful, to feel independent and responsible. When these needs are blocked, children may feel frustrated and engage parents in a power struggle.

Power struggles exist in many forms. In the example above, Bill is striving for power by trying to convince others that he can and will do what he wants, when he wants to do it. At times children will choose to be defiant or stubborn in order to test their limits. Or they may display power passively by resisting or "holding back" when parents attempt to make them comply. In any case, children whose goal is power feel worthwhile only when they are boss. If they do surrender to their parents temporarily, they are likely to come back later with a new power tactic, and with stronger determination.

When parents feel provoked or angry and find themselves arguing in a vicious circle, the goal is usually power. Children whose goal is power attempt to engage their parents in arguments, pushing them to either give in or to fight back continuously. In a power situation, parents struggle with which response to choose.

Conflict is inevitable. In fact, it is a normal and natural part of learning to live together. How we handle conflict is the issue. We must learn how to be both firm and loving without counterattacking or being overly permissive; otherwise we reinforce the misbehavior by cooperating with the child's intention.

It helps to remember in situations like these that nearly every child strives for control at one time or the other and tests every rule to gain a feeling of power. But at a deeper level children actually want limits; when standards are not set and maintained with firm conviction they become insecure and doubtful of their parents' integrity.

One of the best ways to handle power struggles is through recognition. Remember, power struggles grow from a need to feel independent and successful. Children need to gain a sense of self-confidence and freedom to choose what they like through positive encouragement. The more affirmation they receive, the less likely it is that they will strive for power by making unreasonable demands. Healthy self-confidence is built by acknowledging children's accomplishments and helpful contributions. A five-year-old brings home a paper project from school and Mom and Dad say, "Let's see your picture. I like that—tell me about it!" Or a ten-year-old works hard on a project and shows an effort towards self-discipline and Dad responds sincerely, "Can I read your paper when you're finished? I'd like to learn more about that subject."

One of the first responsibilities children need to be taught is how to adjust to the family schedule and cooperate with the family system. This adjustment process competes with their innate drive for wanting others to serve them, and power struggles can and will erupt. Gradually, and with positive motivation, parents have to reject their children's self-centered demands and help them learn to meet their needs in acceptable ways. Knowing how to handle power struggles in the home can help us do this without either losing control or giving in to unreasonable demands.

REVENGE

The afternoon before company was to come, Mom had tried to settle an argument between Frank and his younger sister. That evening following dinner, the resumption of the conflict caused great embarrassment. Frank began by pestering Sue. Mom threatened, "OK, stop it, or you'll be sent to your room!" But before long Frank managed to provoke his sister into another argument, and Dad quickly marched him to his bedroom. "You're mean to me! I hate all of you!" Frank yelled (much aware of the additional embarrassment for his parents, as the entire exchange took place within earshot of their friends). Dad in anger muffled Frank's mouth and gave him a good shaking with a pop on the behind. "Don't you talk to me that way! You know better than that!" He left the room, but within a few minutes had to return to make Frank turn off his blaring radio.

This episode demonstrates the progression of the first three goals of child behavior: attention, power, and finally revenge. Frank continued to provoke his sister in order to get attention. When his parents displayed their anger towards him, they initiated a power struggle which Frank was determined to win. The anger continued, and retaliation from both parents and child kept the vicious cycle going. Many conflicts follow this self-defeating pattern: a need or desire is frustrated, a power struggle results, and then revenge and endless counterattacks follow.

When children pursue a goal of revenge, they are attempting to gain a sense of justice by hurting others whom they feel have hurt them. Children who try to get revenge often have feelings bottled up inside which they don't know how to handle appropriately. They are convinced they are unlovable, and set out to prove it by misbehaving. They get recognition by being cruel, disliked, and rejected; they gain a warped sense of achievement by successfully attacking others.

Like other goals of behavior, the negative goal of revenge is related to the genuine need to belong, to be treated fairly and with justice, to be involved, appreciated, and accepted by family members. When the child feels ostracized or disliked, he may think, "At least I can make them feel sorry for hurting me. I'll show them that I'm smart by getting even with them. I'll frustrate them. Then they'll know how it feels to be hurt, too. If they hate me, then I'll give them something to hate."

In order for a child to learn self-control and respect, parents likewise must demonstrate the ability to not counterattack. To break the cycle of revenge, they will have to avoid using punishment and retaliation. This is an area in which "separating the deed from the doer"—expressing our anger firmly but lovingly, and attacking the misbehavior but not the child—is vital.

INADEQUACY

Eight-year-old Jay was having difficulty in school. In a conference, the teacher told Mother that he was an extremely poor reader, was behind in all subjects, and didn't seem to get anywhere, no matter how much he tried nor how much extra help she gave him. "What does Jay do to help at home?" the teacher asked. "I quit asking him to do things at home," Mother replied. "He doesn't want to do anything, and if he does, he is so clumsy and does it so badly that I just don't ask him any more."

In the above situation, which is taken directly from Dreikurs's book,[2] Jay is completely discouraged; he has given up because he feels that he has no chance to succeed in any way. He uses his helplessness (his exaggerated or imagined deficiencies) to avoid any task where the failure he expects will bring more embarrassment.

Children like Jay live constantly with the fear of failure. They already lack confidence, so they withdraw for the sake of psychological safety. It's as if they were saying, "If I try and fail again you will see how worthless and stupid I really am." They may give up or try to get others to do things for them. Children with a goal of inadequacy operate from a mistaken premise that has been reinforced by a series of discouraging experiences.

Encouragement is the solution when children are pursuing the goal of inadequacy. Criticism tears down confidence and keeps children from wanting to try at all. They need encouragement and affirmation in order to regain a sense of acceptance, love, worth, and self-confidence. Pity only inspires self-pity; criticism reinforces the mistaken concept of helplessness. Only encouragement can enable children to change their mistaken goal.

IT'S YOUR MOVE

Life does look very different from three feet high. Children's feelings and perspectives are different from ours. Misbehavior that baffles and frustrates us may seem perfectly logical to children who are pursuing the mistaken goals of attention, power, revenge, or inadequacy.

When we are aware of these four mistaken goals behind our children's negative behavior, we have a basis for action on our part; we can remove the reward of the misbehavior. Children whose behavior fails to help them reach their mistaken goals have the option to choose more positive behaviors that help them meet their psychological needs in more acceptable ways.

As we try to determine the goals that underlie our children's misbehavior, we must remember that an awareness of behavior goals is a tool, not a weapon. "Putting children in their place" by telling them we know why they are misbehaving could be detrimental. Our understanding of our children's natures and thinking patterns is to be used as a basis for *our* change. Our insight is for enabling us to show understanding and preventing us from being victimized, not for holding over our children's heads.

Understanding goals of behavior will not automatically stop or prevent negative behavior. There are no simple answers to resolving attention seeking, power struggles, revenge tactics, or underachieving. In this chapter we have only begun to suggest appropriate ways of resolving some of these problems.

There will be times when the positive intervention methods listed in this chapter don't work. Then a parent needs to know what use of authority and parental "power" is acceptable and effective in teaching a child obedience, respect for authority, and self-control. The next two chapters will explore the use of discipline and consequences for correcting misbehavior.

11 | *I Love You Too Much to Let You Misbehave*

DISCIPLINING
WITH LOVE AND
AUTHORITY

Most parents want their children to be happy. They want them to grow up creative and loving, self-confident and spiritually alive. Most parents want to be "good parents."

But many mothers and fathers operate under mistaken ideas about what being a "good parent" means. They may believe they are failures as parents unless their children feel happy all the time, and so ignore irresponsible behavior rather than upset a child by disciplining him. Or they may fear "stifling a child's creativity" and end up confusing "freedom with anarchy, self-expression with indulgence, liberty with license,"[1] letting their children run roughshod over others rather than impose limits on their "freedom."

In either case they are bound for heartache. Children do need freedom and feelings of happiness, but they also need discipline. They can't develop healthy self-esteem if they cannot learn to respect limits and to control their own desires. If they are allowed to assume that happiness and satisfaction come only from getting their own way, they will grow up frustrated and bitter, because there will be many times they do *not* get their way. And if they are permitted to satisfy their human potential for sin and selfishness by taking advantage of others (even their parents), they will grow up unloved and unloving.

The point is clear—loving parents who want their children to be truly happy will discipline them. But the wrong kind of discipline can do more harm than good. The following memories, expressed by members of a personal growth group, illustrate the detrimental effects misguided or harsh discipline can have:

> My mom and dad used to punish me for calling people names by locking me in the bathroom with a Bible and making me memorize Bible verses. That's my image of God. . . . No wonder to this day I detest anything that has to do with obeying God.

> My dad used to beat me and quote Scripture at the same time. I really love God deep down in my heart, and I try to pray. . . . But I really have a hard time trying to understand what God and religion are all about.

These comments are similar to many I hear in my counseling practice. One of my clients, a man who can quote many Scripture passages, leads a life of confusion, bitterness, and frustration. He has a brilliant mind, but his spirit has been crushed by the unwise discipline he received as a child.

So there's the dilemma of discipline: "Harsh, oppressive, whimsical, unloving, and/or capricious punishment"[2] can hurt a child emotionally, psychologically, and even spiritually, but unnecessary reluctance to exercise parental authority can also be detrimental. Either extreme can lead to heartache and rebellion in children. So how do parents decide when and how to discipline their children, and how do they avoid being either overly harsh or overly permissive?

This dilemma is often compounded by the fact that husbands and wives may have trouble agreeing between themselves what tactics to take:

> My parents seemed to have a good handle on disciplining me. I learned to respect them, and I know that they really cared for me, so I tried to cooperate. Sure, I tested them a lot and got into hassles with them, but now as I look back, I see that they handled me about the best they could. . . . My problem now is that my husband's experiences were just the opposite. So we disagree on disciplining the children.

It takes thinking, planning, and concern for a family to develop a concerted plan of discipline, to agree on what family rules will be implemented and how they will be enforced. Before we look at any particular methods of discipline, it will be helpful to look at what discipline is, what it should accomplish, and what principles can guide us as we seek a style of loving discipline that will help our children grow up happy and responsible. That is the purpose of this chapter.

THE GOAL OF DISCIPLINE

We discipline children in order to help them learn to choose desirable behaviors in the home and in society and avoid unacceptable behaviors. All families have unwritten expectations of what is acceptable behavior. Children not only need to internalize family value systems, but eventually to be able to choose responsible, worthwhile behaviors and values on their own:

> Train up a child in keeping with his individual personality needs and bent, and when he reaches the age of maturity and responsibility—in which he has to rely upon making his own decisions—he will not depart from the training, example, and motivation he has been given (Prov. 22:6).

The goal of disciplining our children, then, is to encourage their growth as respectful, responsible, self-disciplined individuals. Failure to achieve self-control will result in low self-esteem, and in the failure to show concern and respect toward others. Children can't demonstrate genuine love and understanding without having a sense of respect for themselves and others.

Appropriate use of discipline is not what a parent does *to* the child, but what a loving parent does *for* the child. An appropriate attitude toward a disobedient child is one suggested by Dr. James Dobson in *Dare to Discipline:* "I love you too much to let you behave like that."[3]

A QUESTION OF AUTHORITY

Scripture makes it clear that we as parents have a God-appointed authority over our children, and that responsible parents will exercise this authority. But parental authority, like any other kind of authority, can be abused. Common mistakes parents make in exercising their appointed authority include:

—failing to listen to the feelings of their children
—belittling children with sarcasm and contempt
—embarrassing children in front of peers or adults, especially significantly close relatives
—punishing children in front of or within hearing distance of others
—"snatching up" children and punishing in anger without explaining the reason for the consequence
—being unfair and unreasonable in the kind or amount of discipline
—taking too much responsibility for correcting children's problems when they could learn more by being responsible for their own problems
—preventing children from learning to make their own decisions and, consequently, from learning personal motivation for change
—controlling children by fear and guilt rather than encouraging them to become discerning in their choices

—giving children the impression that acceptable behavior is only necessary when an authority figure is present
—creating a power struggle, causing resistance or even retaliation by forcing children to conform
—ignoring the more effective ways of relating to children—active listening, "I statements," etc.

The key to exercising authority without abusing it is to understand the difference between a style of parenting that is *authoritative* and one that is *authoritarian:*

AUTHORITATIVE	AUTHORITARIAN
Encouraging individual freedom; respected, reasonable, responsible; assertive but not manipulative; decisive, wise, trustworthy.	Repressing individual freedom; strict, harsh, severe, unyielding; dogmatic, tyrannical, uncompromising.

This is an important distinction, one many parents fail to make. Authoritative parenting is based on respect for what is right, while authoritarian parenting is based on the misconception that the parent must always be right. The one cultivates children; the other condemns them. One communicates; the other blames. One helps encourage children toward self-discipline and responsible living; the other hinders that growth. The loving parents' approach to discipline will be *authoritative,* not *authoritarian.*

DISCIPLINE, NOT PUNISHMENT

There is another important distinction that needs to be made—that between discipline and punishment. Discipline is designed to encourage children toward mature responsibility (the style of the authoritative parent). Punishment seeks retribution for misbehavior (the style of the authoritarian parent).

Briefly, the differences between discipline and punishment can be listed as follows:

DISCIPLINE	PUNISHMENT
Builds relationships by correcting the behavior while accepting the child.	Rejects the child who has behaved undesirably; the result is alienation.
Focuses on present learning experience without harshness	Focuses on misbehavior, causing hurt.
Displays anger appropriately—against the deed and not the doer.	Displays anger against the doer, and uses power to gain own way.
Allows for cooperation and mutual respect to develop.	Sets up power struggles, cycles of revenge and counter-revenge.
Motivates by firm kindness and consistency.	Motivates by fear.

Punishment often attempts to secure obedience by sheer force, without love and understanding. This method may seem to work while children are young and can still be controlled by fear and pain, but there is no love cultivated to fill the empty places that remain when misbehaviors are driven out. Punishment may accomplish compliance with the rules, but that is all. And sooner or later the child will be likely to rebel.

It is well to remember that punishment by force can involve verbal as well as physical blows! Wounds to the body may heal, but the injured spirit of a discouraged child may take much longer to find true healing.

Many parents, it seems, rely on punishment as a way of handling misbehavior on the part of their children. The same parents will usually rely on a system of rewards for promoting good behavior. But there are serious drawbacks to using reward and punishment as a system of discipline:

1. It teaches children that "might makes right," that power is the way to get what they want.
2. It focuses on control as the basis of family togetherness. The constant harassment to conform and please the parent can create both self-hate and a desire for revenge.
3. Punishment is often administered to hurt the person rather than solve the problem.
4. Reward and punishment, used selfishly by parents to get their own way, reinforces selfishness in children.
5. Punishment shows disrespect for the personhood of children; it indicates they are inferior and insignificant.
6. Children often use punishment to convince themselves that future misbehavior is justified.
7. Rewards and punishments can lead us to the understanding that acceptance in the family depends solely on performance; this in turn can cause frustration and feelings of inadequacy and rejection.
8. Children may deliberately seek out punishment as a way of getting attention, or they may welcome it as a means of relieving guilt and avoiding responsibility for change. When this happens, punishment fails to accomplish its purpose of discouraging misbehavior.
9. Rewards for good behavior may teach children to behave properly only when they receive pleasure as a result.

The weaknesses of the reward and punishment system are easily seen in American culture today. Our materialistic and manipulative society reinforces the idea that our goal in life is to grab the rewards we can while avoiding getting caught. Moral principles are often short-circuited by the pragmatism of getting by with the least pain and the most profit; this philosophy permeates many of our homes, our businesses, our institutions. We can lessen its influence by downplaying the role of punishment and reward in disciplining children.

THE SEARCH FOR BALANCE

As parents, we need to develop a workable balance between acceptance and firmness when it comes to our children. We need to understand the difference between harsh, selfish punishment and loving, firm, authoritative discipline. Discipline is a process of *motivating a child to internalize principles of self-discipline which will equip him to reach his own self-fulfillment.* But discipline is a learned process, and we need a model to follow. That model can be found in Scripture.

The Bible portrays a balanced approach to discipline— one which I've termed "theocratic-democratic." It is "theocratic" in the sense that each family member finds his place in joyful and loving submission to God and in the correct application of God's Word. Submission is not subordination; rather, it is the acknowledgment of a standard which is believed to be trustworthy and divinely inspired. The biblical view of discipline is also "democratic" in the sense that emphasis is given to the need for mutual respect and love between parents and children. The Bible gives clear instructions as to who is to serve as the authority of the home, but it also encourages acceptance, love, concern, and personal freedom in responsible, cooperative living.

Scripture also gives us a clear model for discipline in its portrayal of God as our heavenly Father who disciplines his children out of love for them. The message of Hebrews 12:5–17 is an expression of this principle:

Have you forgotten the encouraging words God spoke to you, his child, for the fact that he disciplines you is a sign that you belong to and are loved by him. He says, "My son, don't be angry when the Lord corrects or restricts you. Don't be discouraged when you are put to the test or when he has to show you that you are wrong. For the fact that he disciplines you shows that he loves you. The fact that he whips you proves that you are really his child, for whom he cares enough not to let you misbehave or be ruined for life."

Let God train you, for he is doing what any loving father does for his children. Whoever heard of a son who is loved but who is never corrected? If God doesn't discipline you when you need it, as other fathers discipline their sons, then you aren't really God's son at all—you don't really belong in his family. Since we respect our fathers here on earth, even though they discipline us, should we not all the more be glad to submit to God's training so that we can begin to live fulfilled lives?

Our earthly fathers trained us for a few years during our growth in childhood, doing the best they knew how for our benefit, but God's correction is always right and for our best good, that we may share his holiness. Being disciplined isn't enjoyable while it is happening—it hurts. But afterward we can see the results—a quiet growth in grace and character.

This passage, along with other portions of Scripture, imply five major principles of discipline, based on God's model, that we can follow in disciplining our children. The underlying motive is always *love;* we need to learn to discipline with love, and to love when disciplining.

Principle #1: Encourage Honest Questions.

The first principle of God's method of discipline is that he allows, even encourages, honest questions from his children. Throughout Scripture we find graphic illustrations of God responding directly to his people to help them understand the reasons for their testing. The book of Psalms is full of searching questions from the heart, addressed to a God who is considered open to expressions of pain and who understands human limitation. Most of Jesus' teachings began as responses to people who were seeking to understand life's complexities and uncertainties; even those who asked Jesus questions in order to trap him received authoritative and thought-provoking replies. Much of the time Jesus redirected those questions and showed the questioners the real meanings behind their ploys.

As parents, we can also help our children understand what we are trying to teach them by allowing them to raise questions in the right attitude and spirit. Of course, discretion is necessary as Joe Temple points out in his book, *Know Your Child:*

> In following this practice, you must remember that children are smart, and sometimes they will ask "Why?" not because they want to know why, but because they want to postpone doing what you have asked them to do. You have to be wise enough to know when the "Why" is just a delay tactic and when it is a sincere question that needs an answer. Sometimes when they say "Why?" we have to say to them, "We have been over that already and you know why." Sometimes we have to say, "I cannot explain to you right now why; you would not understand. Your daddy has a reason."[4]

We have to consider many factors in deciding how much to let a child question, but we need to maintain an open attitude toward their concerns.

Principle #2: Explain the Reasons.

Isaiah 1:18 begins with God's invitation to "come, let us reason together." God reasons with his children when he disciplines them. Not only does he encourage our questions; he desires that we know the error of our ways and the consequences of our sins. This is a good model for us as parents to follow. We need not only to listen, but to share our understanding with our children in a nonjudgmental, nonsuperior manner.

Children can be very practical and sensible, and taking the time to reason with them is a worthwhile investment. Children can benefit when they understand the rational and scriptural premises behind our decisions. If we never take the time to explain, they will begin to suspect that our values have no basis, or that our decisions are based on guilt, fear, our own desires, or irrational beliefs.

When we reason with our children, there is no need to overexplain; long explanations only create confusion. The most effective method of giving explanations is to relate our reasons with firmness, but in a tone of voice that communicates care and concern. Children may be able to tell what it is about their behavior that is not good; this participation on their part should be encouraged. During the discussion, it is important that children understand the consequences of their actions for themselves, for others, and for God. Whenever possible, it is a good idea to suggest alternate behaviors and choices, especially if the children are tired and frustrated and unable to come up with their own ideas.

Principle #3: Exemplify Consistency.

It is important that our discipline be consistent. Children are often robbed of their confidence and trust in their parents by hit-and-miss methods of discipline. Spouses need to come to an agreement about the standards and rules of the home and enforce them in a way that is clearly predictable to the children. For example, the failure to make up a bed should not be handled one time with a scolding and another time with the loss of a week's privileges. Backtalk should not be ignored one week and punished with a spanking the next.

Being consistent doesn't mean being perfect—no one can achieve that. Being human, we are apt to react to specific situations on the basis of how we feel at the time. But consistency does involve practicing self-control in choosing our reactions to our children's misbehaviors. When we discipline our children consistently, we set an example of what we expect from them.

Principle #4: Enforce Restrictions.

The fourth principle of discipline portrayed in Scripture is that God restricts his children. Implied in Jesus' instructions to be in the world, but not a part of it (John 17), is the reality that there are certain *limitations* as to what is good for the development of character. In *Know Your Child,* Joe Temple explains that one aspect of the word translated "train" in Proverbs 22:6 is "restrict." We have already seen that both children and adults have an inner bent toward selfishness and evil as well as the potential for God-consciousness and good; the latter potential *must* be cultivated and encouraged. Restrictions play an important role in this process.

We don't place restrictions on children for the purpose of sheltering, embarrassing, or irritating them (regardless of what they may say!). Restrictions are guidelines wise parents establish in order to give their children security and protection from temptations that at times can be overwhelming. They should not ignore personal liberty and responsibility, or deny children the chance to learn how to cope with the world, and they must always be made within the context of *clear expectations* and *explained consequences.*

A child will often reply, "But Mom (or Dad), don't you trust me?" and try to make parents back down by making them feel guilty. When this happens, our discernment has to be keen and firm, our response gracious and kind. We must realize that, although children are seldom self-aware enough to express it directly, they really want limits and guidelines. Even when they protest, they are indirectly saying to us:

> "Please be firm with me enough to say no when I need it. There are times when I feel that getting my own way is what will really make me happy. If your experience can help me, then don't give in. Be lovingly persistent with me."

Understanding this, we might explain to our children that there are two kinds of trust. We might reply, "Yes, we trust you, but we don't trust what can happen." Restricting a child does not imply a lack of trust in the relationship; it simply recognizes that we can also "trust" in the fact that human nature, emotions, logic, and will are vulnerable to certain temptations.

What restrictions are necessary to protect and help our children depends on the personality and age of the child, on the circumstances, and on many other factors. As our children grow older and become more responsible, we can decrease our supervision and allow them more room for self-discipline.

Principle #5: Expect Failures.

The final principle in God's model of parenting is that God allows for failure as he disciplines us. Building Christian character involves being willing to learn from mistakes, which are an inevitable part of both child development and "parent development." We grow stronger from learning what *not* to do as well as what to do.

Children certainly need correction, but the pain, confusion, and guilt of failure should never be used to humiliate them or to crush their spirit. At times we need to respond as I once heard a grandmother say to her grandson, "That's OK . . . I'm glad you're not hurt. Broken lamps can be replaced, but you can't be." This doesn't tell the child that he can break lamps indiscriminately; rather it focuses on the fact that he is a valuable person, and that it is all right to fail. Of course, each circumstance needs to be examined in the context of the specific misbehavior and of the child's intentions.

We need to be careful not to set children up for failure. Such accusing questions as "Did you do that?" can tempt him to be defensive and perhaps dishonest in an effort to avoid the expected consequences. Parents can try to get the facts and any possible explanations patiently, without tempting the child to be untruthful.

It is important to avoid implying that making a mistake is a catastrophe. Encouraging parenting and healthy discipline do not assume perfection on the part of either parent or child; they are rooted in reason, honesty, consistency, love, open communication, and—most importantly—trust in God to reveal himself to our children as we exercise authority and discipline.

When a person breaks his arm, an interesting process takes place. The body begins a healing process which builds up a new layer of calcium in the crack, actually causing a lump for a while, because there is more calcium than needed to fill the crack. The healed bone is then stronger than before because of the extra deposit. Failure, like a broken bone, can actually produce greater strength *if* properly treated. That's an encouraging word to parents who are attempting to follow God's model of loving discipline.

WITH GOD'S HELP

Wise discipline, backed with love, produces self-control, self-respect, and mutual respect with others. Children who receive balanced quantities of love and discipline learn the joy of choosing to be unselfish, and of developing healthy attitudes, values, and standards.

But wise discipline, based on God's model, is not something we can accomplish without prayerful intercession. Discipline without prayer loses its impetus; caring firmness and positive guidance all work more effectively when founded in a prayerful dependence on our heavenly Father. His character can be instilled in our hearts, minds, and spirits by his Holy Spirit. We can ask him to keep us in touch with our children, aware of what they need to grow. We are then equipped to communicate genuine love in the discipline of our children.

As we do this, both we and our children can move toward a greater understanding of the truth of God, and the trustworthiness of his Word in revealing what is good for us. And we can grow toward the unique human-spiritual potential entrusted to all who are born spiritually into God's family.

Peter, in his second letter, described this process of Christian growth:

> Seeing that he has given us his divine power so that we might have everything we need for living a good and godly life to the fullest, he now shares his own goodness with us as we advance in the knowledge of him, for he has called us to his own glory and excellence. By his mighty power he has given us all of his

great promises so that we might be partakers of his character and sharers of the divine nature, escaping the moral decay that is in the world because of selfish greed. Now obtain these gifts by diligently making an effort in exercising your faith to develop or add to it . . . courage, knowledge [sound rational thinking rooted in moral change and obedience], personal self-control, patient endurance, godliness [which is a relationship of faithfulness to God and honest integrity with others], caring affection, and Christ's love—the kind which demonstrates itself to everyone (2 Pet. 1:3–7).

12 | *The Ball's in Your Court*

**USING THE
PRINCIPLE OF
NATURAL, LOGICAL,
AND SPIRITUAL
CONSEQUENCES**

Among my favorite childhood stories were those about the "Boxcar Children." A series of books told about the adventures of a family of young children who had to make it on their own. Not wanting to be separated when they were unexpectedly orphaned, they decided to run away. They made their home in an abandoned railroad boxcar, earned money for food by doing odd jobs, and kept their milk fresh by storing it in a cold running brook. They learned to handle almost every circumstance and predicament as they encountered it. The excitement and challenge of having to survive from nature and life taught them to be responsible, creative, and cooperative.

Children in our culture are usually provided for so abundantly and supervised so closely that they lack opportunities for that kind of learning. They are told what to do and what not to do, they are rewarded and punished, but they often are denied the chance to learn through creative exploration, trial and error, and experiencing the results of their actions. But it is exactly that kind of learning that develops the maturity described in Proverbs 22:3: "A prudent man foresees the difficulties ahead and prepares for them; the simpleton goes blindly on and suffers the consequences."

Parents can help their children learn to make wise decisions and encourage them to become self-confident and self-reliant by using a system of discipline that lets them see a cause-and-effect relationship between their behaviors and the consequences of their behaviors. In this chapter we will look in depth at how parents can employ the principles of natural, logical, and spiritual consequences in disciplining and encouraging their children.

WHAT ARE NATURAL AND LOGICAL CONSEQUENCES?

Natural consequences are those that come directly from the laws of nature and life. For example, if Dad leaves the lights on in the car, the battery goes dead; if Mom forgets to turn off the stove, the cake burns; if a child forgets to hold his candy bar out of the reach of his dog, the puppy gets the next bite.

When we discipline through natural consequences, we allow our children to experience directly the results of their irresponsible or unwise behavior. If Sally spends all her allowance in two days, she has to live until the next "payday" without funds. If Bruce fails to come home in time for dinner, he has to fix his own meal from leftovers.

Using this kind of discipline helps our children learn the "logic" of why certain behavior is not advisable. They will tell themselves to avoid the behavior the next time, so that the consequences may also be avoided. They learn to "own" their problems and to make future decisions according to the foreseeable results.

It is not always wise or possible, however, to use natural consequences to discipline a child. The behavior may not be directly governed by a natural consequence, or the natural consequence may involve too much risk or danger. When a natural consequence could cause harm to the child or to others, parents may employ logical consequences that are based on belief systems and cooperative agreements.

To be effective, logical consequences should still be directly related to the irresponsible behavior. For example, if a child loses a library book, he must earn the money to replace it. Or, if a child fails to remain quiet when he is instructed to, he must leave the room and go elsewhere.

Logical consequences help children learn that society and the family have rights and rules, and that others may impose undesirable consequences for them when their behavior is irresponsible or contrary to the system of values under which they live. This form of discipline is extremely useful in helping a child learn to be responsible for his own happiness without violating the happiness and rights of others through selfish behavior. Using logical consequences for discipline reinforces mutual rights and respect, and children learn through personal persuasion that it is more appropriate and satisfying to respect the rules and rights of others than to violate them.

Both natural and logical consequences produce *self-discipline through self-perception*. Using this technique of discipline encourages children to discover that inappropriate behavior is not acceptable and needs to be changed. It also prepares them to understand the principle of *spiritual* consequences, which is an important scriptural truth.

SPIRITUAL CONSEQUENCES

In contrast to the style of our present culture, the Bible teaches us authoritative absolutes of right and wrong. Just as there are physical laws in the universe by which our world operates, so are there specific moral and spiritual laws, instituted by God, by which human beings must operate if they are to reach their full potential. And just as there are consequences to disobeying God's physical laws, there are spiritual consequences that come from disobeying spiritual laws.

In Galatians 6:7–9 Paul writes:

> Be not deceived; remember that you can't ignore God and his truth. You can't escape his inevitable principles of life; a man will always reap just what he plants.
>
> If he sows to please his own wrong desires, he will be planting seeds of evil. He will surely reap a harvest of spiritual decay and death. But if he plants the right things of the Spirit, he will reap the everlasting life which the Holy Spirit will give him.
>
> And let's not get weary of doing what is right, for after a while we will reap a harvest of blessing if we don't get discouraged and give up.

In this passage Paul is distinguishing between Christian freedom and spiritual consequences. He makes it clear that Christian freedom does not give us liberty to indulge in wrong desires or irresponsible behavior, but that it first demands a consideration of spiritual and moral consequences and then releases those who choose to live responsibly in accordance with God's absolutes. As Roy Putnam affirms in his book, *Life Is a Celebration,*

> Our freedom in Christ was never intended to be used as an excuse for irresponsible living. Our freedom leads us to submission and responsibility. Without submission and responsibility, a creative life is impossible.[1]

Christian freedom, then, is a matter of considering the spiritual consequences of disobedience to God's laws, and of considering God's pattern of successful living. There is a *way* to live, spelled out in the Bible, and we suffer when we ignore that way.

As parents, we can translate the truths of spiritual consequences as revealed in Scripture into a family system of written and unwritten rules which can give direction and purpose in life to our children. We can also effectively utilize the principle of natural and logical consequences to help our children choose to become responsible, self-fulfilled adults. The home is the place for children to learn to respect natural, logical, and spiritual consequences.

USING NATURAL AND LOGICAL CONSEQUENCES IN DISCIPLINE

Learning to use natural, logical, and spiritual consequences as the basis of a system of discipline may take some practice. Here are some general principles that can help us increase our accuracy and consistency in applying this technique of discipline:

Principle #1: Avoid Threats.

Threatening unrealistic or severe consequences doesn't earn a respectful *response* or compliance to authority. Threats are neither natural nor logical consequences—they are bids for power. If a consequence is threatened in anger, the child will more than likely be triggered to fight back. And if the threatened consequence is unreasonable or too severe, the parent will be forced to back down and the child will learn to ignore the threats.

Let's look at an example. Joe has missed the bus to school again. Dad is angry, and speaks in a demeaning tone of voice:

> "Well, that's just too bad. I'm not going to take you again—you'll just have to walk to school. Maybe that'll teach you not to be so lazy."

Dad's threatening attitude triggers Joe to fight back, to make excuses, to come up with all sorts of reasons why he *can't* walk to school. And since it's raining very hard, Dad soon realizes he can't back up his threat; he ends up taking Joe to school anyway.

An attitude that demonstrates mutual respect for rights

could help Dad eliminate the power struggle and avoid the tendency to threaten unreasonable consequences. Dad could have said:

> "Joe, that's the second time this week you've missed the bus. I'm concerned that you can't take the responsibility to get ready on time, and it is really hard for me to take you to school and then be on time myself. I'll take you this time, since it is raining, but after this you'll have to work out other arrangements."

This kind of response would initiate conversation in which Dad could prepare Joe for his responsibility and make clear what will be expected of him. A week later, if Joe misses the bus again, he will know that he will have to be tardy and suffer the consequences at school. He also knows that if the weather is reasonable he will have to walk the three miles to school.

In stating consequences, parents need not overexplain, argue, cajole, or rationalize. We should not try to make our children feel guilty or "small" as a means of motivating them toward desirable behaviors. And we should never threaten consequences we are not prepared to carry out.

Our assumptions as to what will cause children to obey are often one hundred eighty degrees removed from what actually motivates a child. Children soon learn the nonverbal cues that tell them when their parents really mean what they say; a common-sense approach with a self-disclosing statement will bring more favorable results than an angry or empty threat. A firm stand and a loving attitude that communicates, "I care too much about my own emotional stress limits and about you and your needs to not help you learn to cooperate and act responsibly; I care too much to let you misbehave and defy authority," will encourage a child toward acceptable behavior.

Principle #2: Allow Choices.

If children are to grow toward self-discipline, they need the chance to make choices about their behaviors and the consequences. Then, if they choose to disobey, they also have chosen to suffer the natural or logical consequences. The more choice that is included in our communications of discipline, the more chance children will have to cooperate with parental authority and leadership.

In the example we looked at above, Dad could have given Joe a choice by saying:

> "Joe, I know that it's hard to get up so early and rush around to get to your bus stop on time, but Mom and I can't do it for you. You can either make sure that you get up on time to make it from now on, or you'll have to drop one of your activities each day, go to bed earlier, and get up fifteen minutes earlier. It's your choice."

Here's another example. Mother is upset because Sue "borrowed" her hairbrush and lost it at school. She says,

> "Sue, you took my brush to school again without my permission. Now you've lost it! So you'll have to pay for it out of your allowance."

In this case Mother is moralizing and using a logical consequence as an angry punishment without giving Sue an opportunity to choose what she will do. A more positive response would be:

> "Sue, you took my brush and lost it. Now that it's gone, how are you going to replace it?"

In such a response, the focus is on the child's personal responsibility, and the consequence is given in such a manner that the child has a choice about her actions and doesn't have to defend herself. Choices that are given in loving firmness and consistency encourage children to take their responsibility seriously, and to know that consequences will follow if they do not.

Principle #3: Take Time:

In some situations, it takes time to give reasonable, well-thought-out options for children to choose to obey. This means that, especially when a child has a recurring problem, parents should hold off making a decision on what response to make until they have had time to consider what logical consequence will be most effective and what the implications of that particular consequence will be.

Giving ourselves time to think before responding makes it much easier for us to develop sensitivity to the whole situation, to assess our own and our children's feelings and needs, and to gain wisdom from depending on God to guide us in choosing the appropriate response. Taking time also gives us a chance to discuss significant problems with our marriage partner. It is good for both parents to agree on a solution, because children will often try to divide them over an issue.

Until we have time to think things over, we can respond to our children neutrally or tentatively. This keeps communication open and keeps us from overreacting, being inconsistent, and later having to apologize. Appropriate neutral responses are:

"We'll see."
"Tell me how you feel."
"I'm going to stop the car and decide what to do about your disobeying me."
"I need time to think about how to handle this problem."

Each situation will dictate its own tentative response.

By giving ourselves time to respond, we choose to discipline ourselves to make the best decision without yielding to the urge to give the "perfect solution" on the spot and often in anger. Of course, once a parent does come to a decision, it is important that it be communicated firmly and consistently enforced.

Principle #4: Spank When Necessary.

There are times when parental discipline may involve

corporal punishment in order to help children learn to respect others' rights and authority. Especially when danger is involved, this type of parental intervention may be necessary. It teaches a child to be open to the knowledge and wisdom of others. Spankings can, *if* used appropriately, reinforce respect for the authority of parents, society, and God. They also teach that pain is sometimes a natural and logical consequence of violating the rules and laws of life. Spankings can be considered a logical consequence when it has been made clear to the child that refusal to obey family rules will result in corporal punishment.

Here are some guidelines that parents can follow in making this kind of discipline effective:

1. Most of the time it is unwise to spank if there is another appropriate consequence available. The effects of spankings are often short-lived. This form of discipline can become habit-forming for parents and can be interpreted by children as demanding only outward compliance to the rules. Parents should try the other options first; then, if the child still refuses to obey reasonable requests, they may have to use corporal punishment to reinforce respect for parental authority.

2. Spanking may be very appropriate when the child's safety is in jeopardy and the child is not fully capable of assuming responsibility for his actions or fully aware of the danger. For example, children playing in the street, reaching for a knife, or attempting to bite another child must be helped by their parents' owning their problems for them. After the spanking, the parents should attempt to provide more appropriate and safe activities for the children.

3. Younger children usually benefit more from spankings than do older children. With very young children, spanking is most effective as an immediate and appropriate first response; they often understand a carefully timed spank better than words because they can easily

connect the behavior with the punishment. It is best to stop corporal punishment, especially for girls, when the child is between the ages of six and ten.

4. Avoid embarrassing the child if at all possible, especially in front of peers, friends, or family. Remove the child from the presence of others to spank him.

5. Controlling tone of voice and degree of anger is important; spanking carries more authority if done without anger, and harshness is often worse for the child than physical pain. However, none of us is perfect, and at times we may strike a child in anger. When this happens, we need to own our anger, to recognize what is going on. Although we don't need to apologize, rationalize, or feel guilty, we do need to learn from our overreactions. Guilt will only cause us to "explode" more often.

6. Use a paddle, ruler, or other object rather than the hand. This practice disassociates the punishment from the person of the parent so that the child does not fear the parent's hand or body. Physical touching in a family should be used for loving closeness and not for punishment. Often, stopping to find the paddle or ruler will give parents a little more time to deal with their anger, and will allow the children to realize the lesson behind the inflicted physical pain.

7. *Briefly* talk to a young child (especially one between the ages of two and six) to remind him precisely *why* he is being spanked and what he did wrong. Tell him that it's going to hurt, and that it is intended to hurt. Tell him that he is loved but that his persistent disobedience cannot be accepted. Separate the deed from the doer.

8. Spank a child hard enough to let him know that it is a serious matter, yet cautiously enough that he is not abused. Only spank him on his bottom—there's plenty of padding there.

9. After the spanking, it may be appropriate to give the child a hug, even if he withdraws or pulls away. But don't hassle him any longer—he's usually had enough.

Any more lecturing or moralizing will negate the effect of the spanking.

10. Talk with other parents and with your spouse about what spanking can accomplish. Modify your views according to what you discover. When possible, both parents can be present during the spanking unless both are so caught up in their anger that they only reinforce the harshness of the punishment.

How you spank is important. There are other principles parents need to consider. Three key resources I've found helpful are James Dobson's *Hide or Seek, The Strong Willed Child,* and his cassette series *Focus on the Family.*[2]

Principle #5: Make Use of Isolation and Deprivation.

Two other kinds of parental intervention that utilize the principle of natural and logical consequences are isolation and deprivation. Like spanking, these methods can be very effective when used wisely and without harshness.

In using isolation as a technique of discipline, it is better not to always send children to bed or force them to sit in a chair. This associates sleeping and resting with punishment and resentment and can lead to trouble later on. (One client told me that he had to sleep sitting up in a chair while in high school and college because as a child he had received harsh spankings followed by isolation in his bed.) There are certainly more effective means of isolation; separating children, sending them to play alone, or sending them to various other parts of the house can be used as logical consequences. Again, the use of choice is important. For example, Dad may say:

> "Johnny, you may stay in the room with us if you are quiet. If not, you will have to leave, or be taken out to be by yourself. Your mother and I need to talk without being interrupted."

Deprivation may involve withdrawing privileges and special treats or removing the use of favorite toys. Most authorities believe that using money as a discipline tool isn't always the best practice, unless forfeited money is referred to as a "service charge"—a fee or logical penalty for failing to be responsible. Nagging children about how much it costs to support them only creates confusion, guilt, and insecurity.

A child *does* need to be taught the value of money and given an appreciation of hard work, saving, and wise spending. And there *are* times when depriving a child of money can be an appropriate logical consequence for irresponsible behavior. But it should be remembered that restrictions are for teaching, not punishing. For example, one of our children was told that it would take one hundred two weeks, or two years, of her allowance to pay for the treatment exercises that she was receiving to improve her teeth. Therefore, failure to be responsible for her part in doing the exercises each day would first result in a warning, then a restriction, and finally the loss of her weekly allowance until she realized the implication of her neglectful attitude on the family budget.

GROWING RESPONSIBLE CHILDREN

Wilhelm Busch once said, "It is easy to *become* a father, but difficult to *be* one." Learning how to use natural and logical consequences as a tool of discipline takes time; it isn't all learned in one quick, easy step. We are people, parents, and families "in process," and the tension of the process keeps us realistic. Both parents and children need time for gradual and natural transitions into using these principles to shape behavior. If a parent attempts to change his total pattern of parenting and discipline overnight, he will become discouraged and will tend to revert to old patterns and habits.

Obviously, some problems and abuses go with the application of any principle of discipline, including the principle of using natural and logical consequences. But using consequences can help our children develop personal responsibility, self-discipline, and respect for the authority of their parents and of society. It will help them to learn self-confidence and self-respect as well as ways to handle their undesirable behaviors.

It is important that parents ask their children for their involvement and help in this process and motivate them to be responsible in helping with it. As children gradually accept responsibility, they begin to enjoy being responsible. If parents can:

—remain open enough in their attitudes and communication to learn *with* their children
—demonstrate respect for the child's individuality and rights
—remain both firm and kind, without giving in to undue pity, permissiveness, or guilt
—avoid turning consequences into power plays or put-downs
—remain out of the way long enough to let consequences have their natural and logical effect
—focus their goal on encouraging independence, self-discipline, and responsible behavior,

then children will learn personal and social integrity, personal and mutual respect. They will become more mature, considerate, self-confident human beings.

13 | *Responsible Parenting Is Positive Parenting*

**FINDING A
PLAN AND MAKING
IT WORK**

In this chapter I want to summarize the basic methods and concepts we've studied in this book and to look briefly at ways we can put our new skills and insights into action.

My thesis has been that the hallmark of becoming a responsible parent is learning to be an encouraging parent, and that the process of responsible parenting is rooted in the personal, spiritual, and marital growth of the parents. As we individually seek to grow and change as whole persons, looking to the model and character of our heavenly Father, we become the persons we need to be and the responsible parents we want to be. Our children, who look to us as models and as resources for encouragement, understanding, love, acceptance, guidance, and security, have an example of growth to follow.

Being responsible parents doesn't mean being *perfect* parents, but it does demand that we make consistent efforts to love and communicate with our children in specific and effective ways. It involves understanding the implications of various parenting styles and, if necessary, changing our negative forms of relating. In this book I have tried to provide some practical steps for helping parents understand themselves, the family process, and their children, and for learning better communication and relational skills.

The following chart summarizes some of the basic methods we've looked at for responsibly shaping our children's behavior. No one method solves all problems, but an understanding and integration of all these will enable parents to use their own discernment and common sense in choosing how to relate to their children under almost any circumstances.

METHOD	GOALS
Being an example	Establishing models for children to imitate
Setting family goals	Building relationships by working together
Understanding and meeting basic needs for growth	Helping children reach fulfillment and full potential
Building a sense of self-worth	Instilling self-respect, acceptance, and confidence
Expressing encouragement	Reinforcing a positive self-identity and desirable behaviors
Using communication skills	Helping children and other family members learn to be effective, responsible communicators and problem-solvers.

Correcting through discipline or natural and logical consequences

Using the various methods of discipline to teach children responsibility

THE FAMILY MEETING OR COUNCIL

Every child and adult has a need for a sense of belonging to a group. The family is the first and most important group for children. If they experience a sense of mutual respect, worth, and significance in the home, they will develop a sense of well-being and security which will prepare them for adolescence and adult life.

One way to reinforce this sense of belonging in the home is to establish regular family meetings or councils in which every family member has a voice. Numerous books that list strategies for establishing these gatherings and recommend procedures for making them work to full advantage are available. The meeting time and content can vary according to the individual schedules and needs, and can be established according to mutual agreement.

Regardless of what approach is taken to family meetings and gatherings, it is important to make time for some form of regular family communication and group sharing. Family meetings promote family unity and provide time for establishing rules, sharing values and goals, making decisions, solving problems, encouraging each other, and resolving conflicts.

POSITIVE PARENTING

In addition to family meetings, family fun times and devotional periods can build communication and relationship experiences into family life, and can play an important part in shaping children's personalities and behavior patterns. Even more important, however, is the general family atmosphere and the tone of daily family interactions.

The most important step parents can take to improve this general family atmosphere is to concentrate on developing a parenting style that is characterized by encouragement. "Catch 'em being good" is a popular phrase circulating today in parent groups and magazine articles, the idea being that instead of constantly looking for "bad" behavior in children we should look for opportunities to praise them when they are good. The general idea is admirable. However, an even more positive approach would be to "catch kids *doing* something, or catch them making an effort,"[1] focusing on behavior rather than "good" or "bad" character. As we have emphasized in several chapters of this book, the difference is strategic.

As we make the effort to change our critical parenting attitudes to positive, encouraging ones, we will begin to see positive changes in our children. Children's self-images and feelings about themselves are strongly influenced by what we communicate to them. Constant faultfinding tends to produce the very results parents want to prevent, because it tears down children's confidence and feelings of worth. On the other hand, children who are encouraged gain self-assurance and a sense of worth in each new task they undertake, and have less need to misbehave.

A positive self-image is necessary for parents as well as children. Parents get discouraged, too, and need to learn how to love and encourage each other daily. Instead of defending their "rights" when they make mistakes, they need to honestly admit their shortcomings and then attempt to change without reinforcing their frustration by feeling guilty. Parents who come to grips with the development and nourishment of their personal growth needs can begin to understand how to help a child acquire a positive self-concept.

Discipline, rules, and standards, reasonably and systematically applied to each situation, help parents maintain their own sense of identity and purpose and give children a sensible framework for building a healthy self-concept.

GROWING TOGETHER

Learning never ends; it is a full-time job for both parents and children. The most effective method for teaching children is through positive family relationships. Clear communication, meaningful involvement and interaction, and caring relationships are the three keys to effective parenting.

As parents, we are working in partnership with God to bring our children from a self-centered lifestyle to a God-centered and other-centered basis for living. The failure to accept our responsibilities will lead to frustration, but step-by-step personal and spiritual growth will make us effective learners and teachers. And prayerful dependence upon God will give us inner resources beyond all we could imagine. God is always our model and source for becoming positive parents.

NOTES

Chapter 1

1. Clyde and Ruth Narramore, *How to Handle Pressure* (Wheaton, Ill.: Tyndale House, 1975), p. 75.

Chapter 2

1. C. S. Lewis, *Mere Christianity* (New York: The Macmillan Co., 1964), pp. 170-171.

Chapter 3

1. Frances L. Ilg and Louise Bates Ames, *Child Behavior* (New York: Harper & Row, 1955), p. vii.

2. Karen Horney, *Neurosis and Human Growth* (New York: W. W. Norton, 1950), pp. 65 ff.

3. This simplification of Maslow's theory is taken largely from Keith Miller, *The Becomers* (Waco, Tex.: Word Books, 1976), pp. 89–103.

Chapter 4

1. John Powell, *Why Am I Afraid to Tell You Who I Am?* (Niles, Ill.: Argus Communications, 1969), p. 12.

2. Craig W. Ellison, "The Roots of Loneliness," *Christianity Today* 22, no. 11 (10 March 1978):14.

Chapter 5

1. James Kilgore, *Being Up in a Down World* (Irvine, Calif.: Harvest House, 1977), p. 63.

2. Dorothy Corkille Briggs, *Your Child's Self-Esteem* (New York: Doubleday & Co., Dolphin Books, 1975), p. 22.

3. Bruce Narramore, *Help! I'm a Parent* (Grand Rapids, Mich.: Zondervan, 1972), p. 126.

4. James C. Dobson, *Hide or Seek* (Old Tappan, N.J.: Fleming H. Revell Co., 1974), pp. 44-45.

5. Haim G. Ginott, *Between Parent and Child* (New York: Avon Books, 1969), p. 50.

6. James Mallory, *The Kink and I* (Wheaton, Ill.: S.P. Publications, Victor Books, 1973), p. 156.

7. Quoted in Mallory, *The Kink and I,* pp. 156-157.

Chapter 6

1. Albert Mehrabian, "Communicators without Words," *Psychology Today,* September 1968, p. 53.

2. Powell, *Why Am I Afraid?,* pp. 50-85.

3. Ibid, pp. 59, 61.

4. Adapted and used by permission of Patsy Worrell, with additional phrases added by Don Highlander.

5. H. Norman Wright, *Communication: Key to Your Marriage* (Glendale, Calif.: G/L Publications, Regal Books, 1974), pp. 73-74.

Chapter 7

1. Roxie E. Gibson, *Hey God, Listen* (Nashville: R. E. Gibson, 1971), p. 38.

2. Ginott, *Between Parent and Child,* p. 40.

3. Other helpful sources are Thomas Gordon, *P.E.T.: Parent Effectiveness Training* (New York: New American Library, Plume Books, 1975); Don Dinkmeyer and Gary D. McKay, *Raising a Responsible Child* (New York: Simon and Schuster, 1973); Robert R. Carkhuff, *The Art of Helping* (Amherst, Mass.: Human Research Development Press, 1973).

Chapter 8

1. William Glasser, *Reality Therapy* (New York: Harper & Row, 1965), p. 13.

2. Ibid, p. 16.

3. Ginott, *Between Parent and Child,* p. 87.
4. Ibid., p. 87.

Chapter 9

1. Dobson, *Hide or Seek,* p. 69.

Chapter 10

1. Rudolf Dreikurs and Vicki Soltz, *Children: The Challenge* (New York: Duell, Sloan, and Pearce, 1964).
2. Ibid., p. 63.

Chapter 11

1. Rudolf Dreikurs, *A Parent's Guide to Child Discipline* (Des Moines, Iowa: Meredith Corp., 1969), p. xi.
2. James C. Dobson, *Dare to Discipline* (Glendale, Calif.: G/L Publications, Regal Press, 1972), p. 15.
3. Ibid., p. 15.
4. Joe Temple, *Know Your Child* (Grand Rapids, Mich.: Baker Book House, 1974), pp. 93-94.

Chapter 12

1. Roy Putnam, *Life Is a Celebration* (Nashville: Impact Books, 1976), p. 122.

Chapter 13

1. This is a phrase stressed by Dr. Roy M. Kern, a professor at Georgia State University.

AUTHORS, BOOKS, AND RESOURCES FOR FURTHER ENRICHMENT

For Parents

Apple, Virginia Gold. *How to Be a Complete New You: Single or Married.* Glendale, Calif.: G/L Publications, Regal Books, 1975.

Augsburger, David. *Caring Enough to Confront.* Glendale, Calif.: G/L Publications, Regal Books, 1973.

Briggs, Dorothy Corkille. *Your Child's Self-Esteem.* New York: Doubleday & Co., Dolphin Books, 1975.

Campbell, Ross. *How to Really Love Your Child.* Wheaton, Ill.: S. P. Publications, Victor Books, 1977.

Chapman, Gary. *Toward a Growing Marriage.* Chicago: Moody Press, 1978.

Dobson, James C. *Focus on the Family* film series. Waco, Tex: Word Incorporated, 1979.

———. *Hide or Seek.* Old Tappan, N.J.: Fleming H. Revell, 1974.

———. *Preparing for Adolescence.* Santa Ana, Calif.: Vision House, 1978.

———. *Straight Talk to Men and Their Wives.* Waco, Tex.: Word Books, 1980.

———. *The Strong-Willed Child.* Wheaton, Ill.: Tyndale Press, 1978.

McGinnis, Alan Loy. *The Friendship Factor.* Minneapolis: Augsburg Pub., 1979.

Mallory, James. *The Kink and I.* Wheaton, Ill.: Victor Books, 1973.

Shedd, Charlie. *Letters to Karen: On Keeping Love in Marriage.* Nashville: Abingdon Press, 1965.

————. *Letters to Philip: On How to Treat a Woman.* New York: Doubleday & Co., 1968.

————. *You Can Be a Great Parent.* Waco, Tex.: Word Books, 1970.

Walker, Georgiana, ed. *The Celebration Book: Fun Things to Do with Your Family All Year 'Round.* Glendale, Calif.: G/L Publications, Regal Books, 1973.

Warner, Gertrude Chandler. The Alden Family [Boxcar Children] Mystery Series. 19 books. Chicago: Albert Whitman & Co.

Wilt, Joy. Can-Make-and-Do Books. 12 books. Waco, Tex.: Word Inc.

————. *Raising Your Children Toward Emotional and Spiritual Maturity.* Waco, Tex.: Word Books, 1977.

————. The Ready-Set-Grow Series. 24 books. Waco, Tex: Word Inc.

————. *Taming the Big Bad Wolves: How to Take the Huff and Puff Out of Twelve Parenting Problems.* Waco, Tex.: Word Books, 1979.

————. *An Uncomplicated Guide to Becoming a Super-Parent.* Waco, Tex.: Word Books, 1977.

For Counselors, Ministers, Leaders

Carkhuff, Robert R., and Pierce, Richard M. *The Art of Helping: An Introduction to Life Skills.* Amherst, Mass.: Human Resource Development Press, 1973.

————. *Helping Begins at Home.* Amherst, Mass.: Human Resource Development Press.

Carroll, Anne Kristin. *From the Brink of Divorce.* New York: Doubleday & Co., Galilee, 1978.

Collins, Gary R. *Christian Counseling: A Comprehensive Guide.* Waco, Tex.: Word Books, 1980.

————. *The Rebuilding of Psychology.* Wheaton, Ill.: Tyndale Press, 1977.

Dinkmeyer, Donald C., Dinkmeyer, Donald C., Jr., and Pew, W. L. *Adlerian Counseling and Psychotherapy.* Belmont, Calif.: Wadsworth Publishing Co., Brooks/Cole Publishing Co., 1979.

Dinkmeyer, Donald C., and McKay, Gary D. *Raising a Responsible Child.* New York: Simon and Schuster, 1973.

Dreikurs, Rudolf, and Soltz, Vicki. *Children: The Challenge.* New York: Duell, Sloan, and Pearce, 1964.

Kern, Roy M., Matheny, Kenneth B., and Patterson, David. *A Case for Adlerian Counseling.* Chicago: Alfred Adler Institute, 1978.

McKenna, David L. *The Jesus Model.* Waco, Tex.: Word Books, 1977.

Matheny, Kenneth B., and Riordan, Richard J. *Therapy American Style.* Chicago: Nelson Hall, 1979.

Narramore, Bruce. *Help! I'm a Parent.* Grand Rapids, Mich.: Zondervan, 1972.

————. *You're Someone Special.* Grand Rapids, Mich.: Zondervan, 1978.

Satir, Virginia. *Peoplemaking.* Palo Alto, Calif.: Science & Behavior Books, 1972.

Smedes, Lewis B. *Love Within Limits.* Grand Rapids, Mich.: Wm. B. Eerdmans, 1978.